DON'T MISS OUT:

The Ambitious Student's Guide to Financial Aid

by

Anna and Robert Leider
21th Edition

55⁴

Cover Design by Bremmer & Goris
Typesetting by Edington-Rand

Care and diligence have been taken in organizing and presenting the data contained in *Don't Miss Out,* however, Octameron does not guarantee its accuracy. This edition contains information relevant to the 1997/98 academic year. The next edition will be available in September, 1997.

Address editorial correspondence to:
Octameron Associates, Inc.
P.O. Box 2748
Alexandria, VA 22301
(703) 836-5480

Address bookstore inquiries regarding purchases and returns to:
Dearborn Trade
155 North Wacker Drive
Chicago, IL 60606
Outside Illinois, 800/245-BOOK
In Illinois, 312/836-4400 x270

ISBN 1-57509-009-0
PRINTED IN THE UNITED STATES OF AMERICA

Table of Contents

Part IV   The Major Money Sources

Part V   The Big Alternatives

Part VI   Special Opportunities

Part I
Useful Things to Know

Chapter 1
Using this Guide

ORGANIZATION OF GUIDE

The sequence of topics in this guide parallels the steps you should take in your quest to finance college. First, you must define your monetary need and second, you must learn how to finance that need. Please don't skip to the scholarship resource chapters and begin firing off appeals for help. For most people, equating the financial aid process with an isolated search for scholarships is an unproductive way to spend time, and the time of the kind organizations offering assistance. Instead, start at the beginning.

In Part I of this guide you will explore the larger trends in higher education finance, as well as learn to separate fact from fiction.

In Part II you will learn the special vocabulary of financial aid. You will meet the players in the financial aid game, and you will learn how to calculate your family contribution—the amount of money your family will be judged capable of contributing to college costs. We will guide you through the entire aid application process and show you how to take charge of each step along the way.

Why is taking charge important?
1. It increases your eligibility for aid.
2. It enhances your chances of receiving all the aid to which you are entitled.
3. It improves the composition of your award—more grants and fewer loans.
4. It gives you a major advantage over those who enter the process passively, without understanding what is being done to them.
5. It gives you a gargantuan advantage over those who drift through the process in complete confusion.
6. It gives you an infinite advantage over those who don't enter the maze at all.

In Part III, you move from fundamentals to more advanced topics. You become a master of the financial aid game—college selection, personal finance and tax strategies. You learn the best moves for two different situations: when college entrance is approaching fast and when college is still years away.

In Part IV, you will meet the major money sources—the colleges, Uncle Sam, and the states. They are the dispensers of billions of dollars. By getting to know their programs well, you will not overlook a single penny that is due you.

Part V introduces you to two major alternatives for financing college costs—your boss, and the US military. The suggestions may not be to your liking, but you should know about them and consider or reject them at this point in the process.

Part VI groups special opportunities. You've already had the meat and potatoes course. Now you are looking for the cake or maybe just the frosting. You'll find sections here for the bright, the career-oriented, the athlete, the graduate student, and for minorities and women. The tips at the end of Part VI bring together many of the ideas developed earlier at greater length. Use these tips as a review.

There is no Part VII. But if there was, it would be an award ceremony where we present you with the title of "Financial Aid Guru."

Chapter 2
Paying for College in the Year 2000

IT TAKES SPECIAL KNOWLEDGE

A college education is expensive. For some families it can be the largest expenditure they will ever make—more costly than the purchase of a new home and with fewer years to make the payments. Even though this may not be what you want to hear, don't throw up your hands and walk away. Financial help is available—plenty of it. But there is more to getting aid than matching a list of scholarship leads to a pile of stationary . It takes special knowledge. For instance:

Knowing Who Gets the Aid. In theory, student aid should go to those who need it most. In practice, assistance is more likely to find its way to those who know how, when and where to apply. By taking charge of the application process, you have an advantage over those who enter the process in a passive mode. That advantage translates into a greater chance of receiving aid, larger awards, and more desirable awards (i.e., awards you don't have to repay).

Knowing About The Buyer's Market. Competition for students, especially top students, is intense. This competition creates opportunities—opportunities you can maximize.

Knowing Basic Personal Finance Techniques. There are investments, gifts, low-interest loans, education bonds, and special lines of credit. When properly used, these techniques can help your cash flow and reinforce the availability of student aid. When improperly used, they will cancel your eligibility for aid. You want to achieve the former and prevent the latter.

Knowing How to Tell Good Advice From Bad Advice. Advice on paying for college is plentiful. But not all of it is good. Some is dated. Some is wrong. And some is tainted by the self-interest of those who offer it.

Special knowledge is what this guide is all about. **Don't Miss Out** will teach you and your family how to formulate your own financial aid strategy—one that will lead you to a good, affordable higher education.

LOOKING FOR COLLEGE MONEY IS A FAMILY AFFAIR

Paying for college is a family affair. Students can't say, "Let my parents worry about it." Parents shouldn't say, "It's my student's problem." Everyone must be involved. The process must be well understood and the search must be started early otherwise two things can and will happen. At best, the family will end up paying more for college than it should, or can afford. At worst, you will make a frantic, unplanned, last-minute college choice that is not in your best interest.

THE BIG PICTURE

The good news is that in 1997/98 nearly $60 billion in student aid will be available. Another bit of good news is that even more money is out there to be had. Uncle Sam's biggest student aid effort, the Stafford Loan, is an entitlement program. That means everyone who is eligible for a loan can get a loan. But it takes an application. As the great Confucius would have said: "Apply forget—no loan you get." Experts have guessed that several billion more could be tapped if the participation rate of those eligible jumped to 100%.

The good news is balanced, as always, with bad news. In 1997/98, student expenses (tuition, room, board, books, fees, and transportation) will total $129.68 billion and while these expenses continue to take large annual jumps, student aid (except for loan money) will level off or even decline.

Take a good look at **Pie Charts A and B**. Note that Uncle Sam, Colleges, States, and Employer-Paid plans are the main sources of student aid. Not private scholarships. Our advice: When you look for financial aid, head for the tables with the biggest plates. Unfortunately, many student aid seekers don't follow this advice. They make the search for crumbs—that small percent of the Student Aid pie which represents private scholarships—their number one priority. NOT SMART!

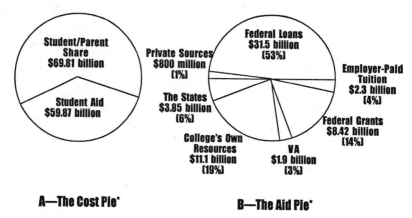

A—The Cost Pie*   **B—The Aid Pie***

Notes to Pie Chart B

    Federal Loans include amounts awarded under the Stafford and PLUS programs, Perkins revolving fund, HEAL and other health professions loans.

    Employer-paid Tuition includes company-based scholarships, tuition reimbursement, and cooperative education programs.

    Federal Grants include Pell, SEOG, SSIG, Work Study, AmericCorps, ROTC, military educational bonuses, military academies, health profession programs, various graduate programs, and numerous smaller programs.

    Veteran's Administration includes the GI Bill and various educational benefits to dependents of veterans.

    College Resources include scholarships, the collegiate share of Work Study, non-subsidized student employment programs, loans from the colleges' own resources, and tuition remissions.

    The States include the state share of federal programs, state grant programs and special loan programs that supplement Stafford and PLUS.

    Other categories are self-explanatory.

    *Figures are all estimated for the 97/98 academic year based on FY97 Budget requests.

LOOKING TO THE FUTURE

Our next point. Paying for college isn't a one-shot deal. You must think in terms of this year's costs, next year's costs, and the following year's costs. If tuition charges strain you now, how desperate are you going to be by the time you are a Senior, and graduating? You must have a sense of all the external factors that can come into play, those that assist you in your effort to meet educational expenses, as well as those that impede you. A lot will happen during the next few years. You should be conscious of these trends and make them part of your continuous, long-range planning. What follows are the most important ones.

TREND A: COLLEGE COSTS INCREASE FASTER THAN INFLATION

Beginning this fall, and continuing over the next 10 years, the number of people going to college will increase from 14.4 million to 16.4 million. This surge means schools should be able to spread their fixed costs—plant, maintenance, staff and faculty salaries—among more paying customers. Combine this with concerted efforts by colleges to cut costs, and the result should be smaller annual tuition increases; we predict a rate just slightly ahead of inflation. Why not a rate equal to inflation? There are many reasons why rising college tuition can't be likened to increases in the cost of bread. For example:

- **Higher education is labor intensive.** For this reason, technological gain does not have as great an impact on "productivity" in the academic world as it does in the industrial world. College students cannot be turned out like Model Ts. Great teaching, as Socrates and Plato knew, comes from conversation between two inquiring minds. Furthermore, in fields such as engineering and computer science, industry provides much higher salary scales than college departments. In consequence, graduate students are turning to industry rather than teaching, and professors keep moving from campus to corporate suites. To fight this trend, colleges must offer more attractive salary packages.

- **State support of higher education is lagging behind costs.** The nation's public schools depend on state appropriations for 60% or more of their support. When state appropriations cannot keep pace with rising costs, these schools must compensate by raising in-state tuitions and skyrocketing their out-of-state charges (it's okay to slip it to out-of-staters: they pay taxes and vote somewhere else).

- **Computermania and Technology.** In their never-ending pursuit of excellence, college after college is grabbing headlines by announcing that every student will be equipped with a personal computer. These computers must be linked by networks and supported by mainframes. They need wiring, cooling, maintenance, and a training staff. All this costs money. Also, if colleges are to be on the leading edge of technology, they must have the latest in laboratories, research equipment, and machinery. Most of them don't have it now. Getting it (and maintaining it) will cost billions. Even a school lucky enough to be "given" a new $40 million lab will need three times that much of its own money to maintain it—unless its wealthy benefactor whose name now adorns the new science center thought to include extra money for custodial services and test tubes.

- **Fuel Costs and Deferred Maintenance.** These are, proportionally, a far greater burden on colleges than on families. Old buildings, drafty halls, and a student population that overloads the circuits with gadgets ranging from hair dryers to VCRs to multimedia computers keep the meters spinning. Also, colleges are plagued with leaky roofs, crumbly foundations, cracking asphalt and inaccessible pipes. Ivy won't hold up the walls forever. Our campuses need over $60 billion in repairs.

- **The Robin Hood syndrome.** Financial aid budgets, with few exceptions, can no longer meet the financial need of all students. For years the common solution was to raise tuition through the roof; those who could pay, in effect, subsidized those who could not. In fact, at some of our nation's pricier, most elite schools, an average of 20% of each student's tuition goes for scholarships for students with need. (Shouldn't families get to deduct this as a charitable contribution?) Slowly, however, as families come to realize how few students

9

actually pay "sticker price," it's putting pressure on colleges to rethink their pricing strategies. Instead of discounting tuition for as many as 90% of their students, some schools are actually lowering tuition for everyone!

- **Graduate Student Subsidies.** Along these same lines, undergraduate tuition often subsidizes the education of graduate students, especially in the social sciences and humanities where grant money is increasingly scarce.

- **Price vs. quality.** While many families are growing uneasy over rising tuitions, our country's 50 or so most competitive colleges still find an abundance of students (and parents) who judge quality by price; the greater the price, the higher the perceived quality, and the greater the applicant pool.

- **Price fixing.** For 35 years, many of our most prestigious schools met to agree on the amount of aid they would offer to their common (overlapping) applicants so students could select a college based on academic needs rather than economics. It also prevented bidding wars for the top students, which in turn, preserved financial aid funds for truly needy students. Families, however, saw it differently. In their eyes, this process denied them all the aid to which they were entitled. More importantly, it assumed they were unable to make decisions about what was and was not important to them in selecting a college. If price was a factor in that decision, then it was the family's right to have a choice of aid packages. For two years, the Justice Department investigated these "Overlap Schools" on possible antitrust violations. The charges have since been dropped, and a settlement negotiated. Essentially, schools agreed not to collaborate on financial aid awards or to discuss prospective tuition rates. And as predicted, the bidding wars have begun (Trend C).

- **Recruiting Costs.** Visiting high schools. Providing toll-free phone numbers. Designing and maintaining ever-hipper web sites. Printing and mailing glossy color viewbooks. Hosting campus visits for students as well as counselors. Recruiting costs at private four-year institutions now average over $1,500 per student enrolled. At four-year public colleges, that cost is a mere $700.

- **Comparison shopping.** As students and parents become more sophisticated shoppers, they expect more for their money. They expect colleges to provide ample sports and recreational facilities, adequate levels of campus security, health care facilities (complete with resident psychologists, psychiatrists and drug/alcohol abuse counselors), and extensive career placement offices. Rooms must be wired for computers, hair driers and stereos. And dining halls must accommodate a variety of dietary requirements. All of this costs money. The irony is, that the very people who complain about rising college costs are in part responsible for urging tuitions upward.

- **College is less expensive than most people think.** Not all colleges cost $30,000 a year. In fact, 45% of all students go to community colleges, where annual tuition averages about $1,200 and another 30% attend state universities, where annual tuition averages under $3,000. Even most private colleges charge you less than $10,000. Add $7,000 for room and board, and for what amounts to $40/day at a public school or $70/day at a private one, you get a room (including heat, water and electricity), three meals a day, professional health care, recreational facilities, a wide range of social and cultural activities, counseling services, career assistance, and an education.

TREND B: TUITION PRICE WALL
Families can afford only so many loans, while state and federal governments can

fund only so many grants. The only other way to keep college affordable is for colleges to lower their costs. Fortunately many colleges recognize they can no longer just fiddle around with tuition rates and pricing strategies, but must do more to control their costs. Michigan State has declared a cap on tuition increases (not to exceed inflation). Bennington (traditionally one of our nation's most expensive colleges) has undergone major restructuring to reduce tuition by 10% over the next five years. In fact, about 80% of our nation's colleges are taking lessons from corporate America (or is it Dilbert?) for help in improving their operations. Business buzzwords like "downsizing," "rightsizing," "repositioning," "benchmarking," "outsourcing," and "reengineering" have become campus mantras as schools find ways to live within their means. With personnel costs making up nearly 70% of some collegiate budgets, what this really means is lots of layoffs, buyouts and early retirements. (Or, as they say in the business world, the "release of resources" or increase in "career-change opportunities.") Is this a sign that with top colleges now costing around $30,000 per year we're finally hitting a price wall? Let's hope so! Otherwise, no matter how wise a financial aid consumer you become, private colleges may soon become unaffordable for most middle income families.

TREND C: BIDDING WARS

How do you feel about the car buying process? Do you feel as though every one else gets a better price? Or do you feel pretty confident that you've beaten the salesperson at his or her own game? Some of us will do just about anything to avoid haggling over a price, and feel very badly that some financial aid administrators have been put in a position where even the wealthiest parents and students feel as though it's their right to negotiate for more aid. Unfortunately, the process of awarding financial aid based entirely on "need" is now more of an ideal than an actuality as more and more schools use tuition discounts (or "merit scholarships") to meet recruiting goals. This flexibility in awarding aid has led to a deal making mentality which truly has the potential to corrupt the equalizing powers of higher education. As The *Washington Post* editorialized, those who are more sophisticated or better advised will haggle while the less connected or less confident will not. This cleavage between the "information haves" and "information have-nots" is doubly dangerous when located at the very gateway to education-based upward mobility. We'll have more to say about negotiating aid packages in Chapters 6, 7 and 9.

TREND D: YOUR FICKLE UNCLE SAM

Uncle Sam is the main dispenser of student aid. But Uncle changes his programs every year; sometimes, twice a year. His programs expand and shrink in dollar volume. Money that is authorized may never be appropriated. Money that is appropriated can be rescinded. Eligibility for the programs is as variable as the dollars. In Year A you may be eligible. In Year B you are out. In Year C you are in again—but for a different amount of aid.

This instability is not limited to dollars. It also extends to their delivery. Forms may be late. Deep questions must be resolved on such matters as how to verify selective service registration and citizenship status. The academic year may have started, the dollars appropriated, but the machinery for delivering the dollars is still being tuned.

To complicate matters, Uncle still faces a $4.9 trillion debt and $140 billion budget deficit, about half what it was during the Reagan years, but large enough for Congressional leaders to go berserk. Right now they're trying to solve the deficit problem by slashing every social program on the books, including student aid (while promising tax cuts and keeping B-2 bombers). The Administration has vetoed many of these short-sighted bills, and with 1996 a Presidential election year, you can be sure the power struggle (and the rhetoric) will keep getting nastier.

As a second part of the budget battle, Uncle's giving less money to the states for education, resulting in similar instability at that level as well.

Uncle needs close watching. To watch him intelligently, you must develop a working acquaintance with "authorizations," "appropriations," "budget reconciliations," and "rescissions." Better still, read the new edition of this book which comes out every fall. We'll do the Uncle-watching for you.

TREND E: COLLEGES WANT YOU

Colleges want you. For all but about 100 schools, selectivity is out the window. Today, 92% of all students are accepted by one of their top two college choices. It's a buyer's market. It widens your opportunity to shop wisely and well. And the more marketable you are—good grades, leadership, musical talent, athletic ability—the more college-sponsored financial aid opportunities you will find.

One caution: Under pressure to recruit students, college materials keep getting slicker. Some use advertising, direct mail, and phone solicitation. Many have turned to the Internet for a more direct sales pitch via the Web. Don't be too critical of schools for these practices. Their survival may be at stake. But do raise your consumer guards and evaluate collegiate mass-marketing techniques with the same objectivity and skepticism you reserve for television advertisements and mass-marketing techniques from other sources.

TREND F: CASH FLOW PROBLEMS—CASH FLOW HELP

When tuitions rise faster than available student aid, families must make up the difference. But this is not a "vive la difference" to be cheered. It is a nasty cash flow problem which, in case you don't understand, is what happens when you have the money to pay the bills, but the money is not "liquid." It is tied up in assets like your house, and you certainly don't want to sell your house just to pay the college bills.

But take heart. Problems create solutions. Financial innovators are coming up with plans that will help with the cash flow without requiring you to place a "For Sale" sign in front of the family castle. A lot is going on. And, we'll cover it elsewhere in this guide, just about the time you throw up your hands and say, "We can't do it. No way." We figure this will come around Chapter 7.

TREND G: FASCINATION WITH EXCELLENCE

Major studies have aroused public opinion about the decline of excellence in elementary and secondary schools. Nearly every proposed solution requires tons of money. Lengthen the school day. Lengthen the school year. Pay some teachers more than others. Pay all teachers more. Make everyone wear uniforms. Build single sex schools. Plug a computer into every socket. Put a computer in every home. Not all solutions will be adopted. But some will, and money will flow. While a nation of literate, math whizzes sounds wonderful, in a finite economy, that money must come from somewhere. Most likely, it will come from money that otherwise might have gone to financing your higher education.

But again, there is a upside. The enshrining of excellence legitimizes the use of academic scholarships, on the part of colleges, to attract high-performance students. Expect continued growth in such awards.

TREND H: THE WEB IS NOT A MEDIUM, IT'S A LARGE

More and more college information is showing up on the Web. Nearly 1000 four-year colleges maintain home pages containing everything from virtual campus tours to virtual course catalogues to virtual alumni news. You may also find links to student home pages, letting you "meet" potential classmates. And you can sometimes follow a school's athletic teams, read its student newspaper, or visit the campus art museum. To find a school's address in cyberspace, use a search engine like Yahoo (http://www.yahoo.com) and look up the category, Education: Colleges and Universities. Quite often you'll find the school's web address is simply its name, for example, http://www.brown.edu.

For an overview of all the financial aid information in cyberspace, spend some time with Mark Kantrowitz at http://www.finaid.org. His site links to numerous resources including student aid publications, student aid organizations, scholarship databases and contact information for financial aid offices.

To become a cyberspace activist, try the Alliance to Save Student Aid (http://student-aid.nche.edu), the United States Student Association (http://essential.org/ussa), or the National Association of Graduate and Professional Students (http://www.nagps.org/NAGPS/nagps-hp.html). This last site is updated most frequently, and is useful for undergrads as well.

Throughout this book we've included Web addresses where appropriate, but like snail mail addresses, they can change frequently (and unlike snail mail, they are not reachable if so much as a "~" or a "/" is out of place). Your best bet is to visit Mark Kantrowitz (see address above) and learn to use one of the many search engines to pinpoint the company or type of information you need.

TREND I: A COLLEGE EDUCATION STILL PAYS

A college education will prepare you for a fulfilling life—through broader cultural awareness, deeper knowledge, greater self-confidence, sounder health, richer pleasures, keener citizenship and vastly expanded resources for personal happiness. But if philosophical reasons aren't enough, you'll be pleased to learn that college still helps you stay employed and earn more money. Here are some recent figures from the Census Bureau (adjusted for inflation). Please note: These are averages; women should subtract about 25%, and men should add about 25% to get a more realistic idea of what you can expect to earn!

Highest Education Completed	Average Annual Income	Unemployment Rate
< High School	$12,809	13.5%
High School	$18,737	7.7%
Some College	$24,398	5.9%
College	$32,629	2.9%
Master's	$40,368	N/A
Doctorate	$54,904	N/A
Professional	$74,560	N/A

HOW THE RICH GET RICHER

Children from wealthier families are more likely to go to college. Those with a college education earn more money. Children from wealthier families are more likely to go to college. Those with a college education earn more money. Children from wealthier families are more likely to go to college. Those with a college education earn more money. And so it goes.

Chapter 3
Common Myths & Misconceptions

Practically everyone we know equates the search for monetary help for college with a search for scholarships. Get rid of that belief quickly! And repeat after us three times: To obtain financial aid, sophisticated families:

- Present the family's situation for need analysis in a favorable manner.
- Apply to all the major assistance programs for which they are eligible.
- Apply early, accurately and honestly.
- Select colleges that are most likely to present them with a good aid package.
- When appropriate, discuss with the financial aid administrator the possibility of improving the aid that was offered.
- Become knowledgeable about favorable options—commercial or otherwise— for financing educational expenses not covered by aid awards.

These steps can be worth thousands of dollars. Any other approach will make you the unknowing looking for the unfindable. To avoid wasting time and money, read this chapter on the myths that envelop the financial aid field. And remember: You don't profit from these beliefs; only the people who sustain them do.

WON'T A SCHOLARSHIP REPLACE MY MONEY?

Most people believe that scholarships put money in their pocket. Example: You have been assessed a $5,000 per year contribution to College X, a school that costs more than that to attend. One lucky day, you win a $1,000 scholarship. You now say your contribution will be $4,000. Right? Wrong. Your contribution will still be $5,000. Most colleges take the $1,000, add it to your available family resources, and take away $1,000 of the loan or grant or work opportunity that it had planned to give you. In other words, scholarships can help pay your college bill, but they do not necessarily reduce your share of the bill.

Question: If that is so, then why do clubs and organizations work so hard to raise scholarship money to help a particular student? **Answer**: They are not familiar with financial aid packaging techniques. If they were, all that money raised by candy bar sales and church suppers would go to a different purpose.

Question: Why do colleges urge students to find scholarships? **Answer**: Your scholarship frees collegiate aid the school can now use to help another student. In other words, Student A's scholarship actually benefits Student B. This may not have been the donor's intent, but it is a generous act and should not go unthanked. Remember: Only the money goes to the other student. You retain the honor of having won the scholarship.

LOOKING FOR SPECIAL SCHOLARSHIPS

Every day we get letters from people who tell us their life stories and then ask "is there a special scholarship for me?" These letters sadden us, because we know the writers haven't followed the smart route for getting financial aid. Most financial aid comes from Uncle Sam, your state, or your college and is based on need. If college costs more than your assessed contribution, you are eligible for aid. Your age, sex, race and career ambitions have nothing to do with it.

14

Even if you do find a "special scholarship," remember, there's a big difference between being eligible and winning. For example, your odds of winning a 4H award (250 awards, 500,000 seniors as 4H members), are only 2000:1. To increase your chances, you could purchase a one-week old piglet, feed it 20 times a day until it weighs 1700 pounds. Then rent a forklift and a truck, take it to the state fair, and hope it wins a blue ribbon in the heavy hog competition. This might improve your odds to 20 or 30 to 1. But what about the costs of raising a 1700 pound porker?

Think we're kidding? The Alliance for Young Artists & Writers offered these statistics from its last Art & Writing Awards contest: Students submitted 250,000 art and writing entries. Of those, 12,000 writing and 14,000 art entries went on for national judging with five writing and five art entries each receiving $5,000 scholarships. In other words, odds of winning, 25,000:1. **Our advice:** Go the traditional route first. Then, if you have nothing else to do, and you need practice filling out applications, and you want to help the Postal Service stay in the black, start looking for a "special scholarship." You may even find one.

UNCLAIMED SCHOLARSHIPS

Q. I've read that millions in scholarships goes unclaimed every year. Is this true?

A. This claim is usually made by computerized scholarship search companies who hope you will send them $25-$200 to find those millions. We're sure a few scholarships do go unused every year, but for once, would like to see companies citing these vast untapped resources provide some concrete examples. According to most financial aid professionals, the millions you hear about are unused employee tuition benefits. See below.

MONEY FROM FOUNDATIONS & CORPORATIONS

The College Board estimates that private foundations and corporations give out nearly $8.1 billion in aid, but it's not money you apply for directly. Foundation money mainly goes directly to universities where it's used to help students at the doctoral or post-doctoral level. There is some foundation money for undergraduates, but that money usually has narrow local restrictions, e.g., for students in Teenytiny County. Such grants are well publicized in the local paper.

Corporate money usually goes to employees or children of employees, either in the form of tuition reimbursement or company scholarships. Some corporations do give money to students whose parents aren't on the payroll, but this is usually done via grants to colleges; the colleges in turn select the recipients—you can't apply for them directly. The UPS Foundation, for example, provides nearly $1.6 million each year via 599 different private colleges and universities.

COMPUTERIZED SCHOLARSHIP SEARCHES

If you need information on federal or state student aid, don't pay a computer service. You can learn all you need to know from this book or the free pamphlets published by Uncle Sam and your home state. *If you need information on collegiate student aid,* don't pay a computer service. The college will tell you what you need to know. *If you need information on scholarships offered by your employer or church,* don't pay a computer service. Ask your boss or minister. *If you need information on local scholarships,* don't pay a computer service. Check the HS bulletin board.

Most experts agree, computerized search services seldom help you find private aid. At their very best, they might provide you with a few leads, as opposed to actual dollars; but we've heard too many horror stories of families being duped out of processing fees to recommend this route to anyone. Federal investigations shut down many shady dealers every year, but anxious parents make an easy target, so a new crop of mail fraud perpetrators springs up every year.

Are there any exceptions? Yes, if your state, or college, or high school has a service you can use for free or a small fee (you should NEVER pay more than $50). Also, if you have internet access, you can do a free search of nearly 200,000 sources thanks to fastWeb (http://www.studentservices.com/fastweb).

INCOME SHIFTING DOESN'T PAY

Many people can't accept the fact they are in a higher tax bracket than their children. They will shift assets from themselves to their offspring, thinking the income from these assets will then be taxed at a much lower rate. Sometimes they even construct elaborate trusts with the help of lawyers and accountants whose fees can run upwards of $1,000.

But oftentimes, all this maneuvering is for naught. Investment income in excess of $1,300 for children under 14 is taxed at the parent's rate. Tax rates for trusts can be higher than tax rates for most families. And student assets are assessed at a much high rate than parent assets in determining a family's expected contribution to college costs. In short, some schemes should carry a big red warning label that says, "Income Shifting Can Be Hazardous To Your College Bills." You'll understand better after you read Chapters 7 and 8.

READING THE WRONG REFERENCES

Everybody knows the Consumer Reports' Income Tax Guide takes a somewhat different slant to its subject than publications from the IRS. Consumer Reports' objective is to show you ways to save on taxes while the IRS seeks to extract the last drop of blood. You may value the IRS guide for its mechanical instructions, but not for its substantive advice on holding on to more of your money.

So it is with paying-for-college guides. Before you use one, make sure you know its origin. Is it written from the viewpoint of those who pay the money (parents or students)? Or from those who get the money (colleges or collegiate organizations)? Or those who give the money (Uncle Sam and the states)? The guides may treat the same subject, but their treatment could be many dollars (your dollars) apart.

"READING" ON-LINE REFERENCES

While some of the best "InfoBahn" resources are education-oriented, remember, there is no virtual editor checking facts and biases, so if at all possible, try to identify the information source and heed the warnings above. Also, on a recent browse, many of the sites which boasted helpful names turned out to be scholarship search firms. Avoid them (except for fastWeb mentioned earlier).

READING OLD REFERENCES

When it comes to student aid, any reference older than one year is out of date. If you use an older reference, you will be badly misled with regard to loan sources, subsidies, interest rates, eligibility, grants size, saving techniques, government regulations, and college costs. Even web sites, which should be easy to keep current, frequently have very dated material. Look for the tag line showing when the page was last updated. This wisdom is especially true for students starting school in the 1997/98 year as reauthorization of the entire Higher Education Act looms near!

16

Part II
The Fundamentals of Financial Aid

Chapter 4
Definitions & Players

SHORT DEFINITIONS

Grants and Scholarships are aid awards that do not have to be repaid. They are gifts, however some will require you to perform a service. The recipient of a band scholarship, for instance, may have to dress up in a costume complete with spats, march around a football field, and blow into a tuba whenever the college so directs.

Loans are sums of money that must be repaid. To qualify as financial aid, loans must carry a lower interest charge than prevailing commercial rates. They must also offer favorable repayment provisions. For example, in the Stafford Loan program, borrowers do not start paying interest on the loan nor do they have to retire any of the principal until after completing their studies.

Work-Study counts as financial aid when employment is arranged for you through the financial aid office. Earnings from work you found yourself are not included as part of financial aid. Such earnings are added to the sum you are judged capable of contributing to college costs.

Enrollment Status impacts on aid eligibility. To qualify for most federal aid, you must be at least a half-time student. Half-time is generously defined. It consists of six semester or quarter hours per academic term for schools on the semester, quarter, or trimester system; or 12 semester hours or 18 quarter hours per school year for schools that use a credit hour system. Also under this system, the amount of your award changes with your status. A $1,000 award for a full-time student becomes a $750 award for a three-quarter-time student (one majoring in the waltz?) and $500 for a half-time student. **A tip:** If you are a part-time student and wish to qualify for more aid, take one additional course each semester.

Accreditation is a process that ensures the school's programs meet at least a minimum level of quality. Make sure your school has been accredited by a nationally recognized association. Not only do you not want to waste your tuition dollars getting a worthless education, but students who attend a nonaccredited school will not qualify for federal or state student aid.

Eligible Program is one that leads to a degree or certificate and meets other "integrity" rules established by Uncle Sam. To get federal aid, you must be enrolled in an "eligible program." Students working toward associate, bachelor, professional or graduate degrees need not worry about what constitutes an "eligible program." Students looking at proprietary schools (for a two month study, for example, of computer repair) should take heed. Most student aid fraud takes place in vocational programs of less than two years, and Uncle Sam is trying his best to separate the wheat from the chaff (shaft?). Note: Schools that receive more than 85% of their funding from federal student aid programs are immediately suspect.

18

THE 1ST PLAYER—THE STUDENT

Financial aid programs define students by dependency status. They are either dependent students or independent students.

A dependent student is one who is at least partially dependent on his or her parents for support. The income and assets of both student and parent are used to develop the amount a family must contribute to college costs.

An independent student is not dependent on parental support. Only the student's income and assets (and that of any relevant spouse) are evaluated to determine contribution to college costs. An independent student may also be classified as a dislocated worker as defined below ("The 2nd Player—The Parents"). To be considered independent, under federal regulations, a student must meet one of the following conditions:

1. Be 24 years of age by December 31 of the award year (e.g., December 31, 1997 for the 1997/98 award year).
2. Be an orphan or ward of the court.
3. Be a veteran of the Armed Services.
4. Be married or have legal dependents other than a spouse.
5. Be a professional student, or a graduate student.
6. Be judged independent by the financial aid administrator based on documented unusual circumstances.

Establishing independence can give you an advantage: By not having to include parental income and assets on your financial aid application forms, your college contribution will most likely be lower and that will result in more student aid.

To preserve scarce aid funds, most states and almost all colleges have gone beyond the federal test to impose additional restrictions on your declaration of independence. These include written proof that your parents (or even grandparents) cannot provide any support whatsoever. This is especially true for students who are "independent" according to Uncle Sam's definition, but who have moved back home with mom and dad to save some money.

THE 2ND PLAYER—THE PARENTS

Parents may be loving, caring, supportive role models. The financial aid process doesn't care. Its main interest: Are they married, separated, divorced? Is there a stepparent around who can foot the bill? Here is the impact of marital status on financial aid:

Both Parents Are Alive and Married to Each Other. The income and assets of both parents are fair game for the financial aid computer.

Parents Are Divorced or Separated. The federal financial aid form is only interested in the income and assets of the parent with whom the student lived for the majority of the twelve months preceding the date of the application.

A Parent Remarries. If the parent with whom the student lived the greater part of the twelve months preceding the date of the application remarries, the stepparent's income and assets are evaluated for a contribution to college costs just as though he or she were a natural parent.

These rules apply to federal aid and, generally, to state aid. The colleges, when deciding how to dispense their own money, are not bound by these rules. They can probe deeply into the resources of the divorced or absent parent who got off scot-free under federal regs.

The financial aid process also cares about the parent's employment status. In determining a family's eligibility for aid, aid administrators give special consideration to "dislocated workers." For example, they may recalculate family contribution using expected income, rather than prior year income. If you fall into this category, it's your responsibility to let the financial aid administrator know! In general "dislocated worker" refers to an individual who has been:

1. Fired or laid off (or has received notice of termination), or
2. Unemployed for a long period with little chance for reemployment in the same or similar occupation in the area where he or she resides, or
3. Self-employed (including farmers) but now unemployed because of a natural disaster or poor economic conditions within the community.

THE 3RD PLAYER—THE COLLEGES

Colleges can be classified as either private or public.

Private colleges can be more innovative in developing attractive financial aid packages and tuition assistance programs. They are not as circumscribed by red tape as are tax-supported schools. Private colleges also have more latitude in how to spend their money. Again, it's their money, not the taxpayer's (this also means they're apt to pry more deeply into your family's finances as they try to decide who is most deserving of limited aid funds).

Public colleges, being tax-supported, are usually less expensive. As a general rule, students seldom pay more than 30% of the actual cost of education. The state pays the balance. Also, public colleges have two sets of fee structures: a lower one for state residents and a higher one for out-of-staters. At one time, it was easy to establish state residency to qualify for the lower rate. Today, it's more difficult. Most states have created elaborate bureaucracies, the efficiency of which appears to be judged in direct proportion to the number of residency denials issued.

One more thing. Private and public colleges have no great love for one another. The lack of affection is rooted in money. The privates resent the subsidies that permit the public schools to offer lower tuitions. They would love to end this "unfair competition" by qualifying for subsidies of their own. Moreover, they see their own turf invaded when public schools, not fully sated by subsidies, seek funds from philanthropies that let them get around the inflexible expenditure guidelines imposed by the states. The public schools, for their part, resent the infusion of state money into private college coffers, especially if the state's commitment to its public schools has diminished. Furthermore, they're tired of all the bureaucracy. Some of the wealthier state schools have tried to escape the red tape by privatizing themselves.

Most of this hostility ends when the two must present a united front to fend off repeated efforts to slash the federal education budget.

THE 4TH PLAYER—FEDERAL NEED ANALYSIS SERVICES

Before a college can consider you for aid, it must know how much you can pay. Families that can pay $10,000 won't be eligible for as much as families that can spare only $1,000. Determining how much you can pay without becoming a burden to your neighbors is called **Need Analysis**. Public and private schools now use what amounts to two varying systems.

The process for determining eligibility for federal aid begins with a longish form called the Free Application for Federal Student Aid (FAFSA). Uncle Sam prints 35 million FAFSAs each year, and contracts with several regional processing systems to send data from your completed FAFSA to a central processing system. More will be said about FAFSAs in Chapters 6, 7 and 10. Here we'll just summarize the path your FAFSA takes so you know which computer to blame for each delay you experience! (Last winter, 900,000 applications were delayed by about two months thanks to processor snafus.)

1. You send your completed FAFSA to your regional application processor (that address will be on your FAFSA).
2. The regional processor scans your data and transmits it to the central processor.
3. The central processor matches your application information against several national databases to verify your eligibility for aid. For example, it checks your Selective Service status, your Social Security number, and your citizenship status.
4. The central processor checks your data for inconsistencies and contradictions.
5. The central processor evaluates your finances and calculates your "Expected Family Contribution" (EFC).
6. The central processor incorporates your EFC into a multi-part eligibility document called a Student Aid Report (SAR).
7. The central processor sends you a copy of your SAR.
8. The central processor transmits your data to schools as designated on your FAFSA.
9. The central processor transmits your data to your state higher education agency.

Because the formula used to calculate your EFC is mandated by Uncle Sam, it is known as the Federal Methodology. And since all EFCs are calculated by the same computer, you gain nothing by submitting your FAFSA to one application processor over another. So why are there different processors? To spread out the work load (and the federal contracts).

THE 5TH PLAYER—THE COLLEGE BOARD AND COLLEGE SCHOLARSHIP SERVICE

The process of determining eligibility for collegiate aid is another story. Why? There is no uniformity. Many colleges insist on additional knowledge about your family's finances to determine eligibility for their own programs. The College Board/College Scholarship Service used to collect this information for them on the Financial Aid Form (FAF). Last year, the College Board replaced the FAF with what looks to be a lucrative (and potentially more valuable) product called Financial Aid PROFILE. The core of PROFILE is similar to the old FAF, but the College Board will customize each form with additional questions as required by the colleges to which the student is applying for aid. If it works (i.e., if colleges pay for the service), students will no longer have to file separate institutional aid applications. If it doesn't work, students will be stuck answering more questions than ever before. You'll learn more about PROFILE in Chapter 6. For now, just remember, it's important to find out which schools require what forms to make sure you're considered for every aid source possible.

THE 6TH PLAYER—THE FINANCIAL AID ADMINISTRATOR

For college students, the financial aid administrator can be the most important person on campus. The FAA can take the family contribution and—ouch—increase it or—hooray—reduce it. The FAA can draw from money under the college's direct control or certify the student's eligibility for money not under the college's control. The FAA can decide on the contents of the student's aid package. Is it to be grants the student will not have to repay? Or will it all be loans? In short, the FAA is the final arbiter of how much the family must contribute to college costs and how much outside help, and of what kind, the family will receive.

Unfortunately, FAAs are working under increasingly stressful conditions. At most schools, they have no real say in setting tuition rates, developing operating budgets, or establishing enrollment goals (in terms of numbers or diversity), yet their offices are under constant pressure to make certain enough of the "right" students can afford tuition so the school meets its enrollment goals and balances its budget. The admission office wants to know why musical Johnny didn't enroll (would an extra $2,000 have done the trick?) while the budget director wants to know why needy Dee Dee got $3,000 when splitting that money between no-need, no-show Joey and low-need, no-show Marky would have brought in twice the tuition. To add to this stress, FAAs must keep their aid decisions ethical and consistent and make certain their schools don't run afoul of one of the 7000 sections of Uncle Sam's Higher Education Act.

So why do people become financial aid administrators? A recent look at some top ten lists revealed the following:

Ten—No salary cap like in the NBA and NFL.
Nine—Enjoy watching students cry.
Eight—More acronyms than the military.
Seven—Doing my part for the Paperwork Reduction Act.
Six—Can order all the FAFSAs I want.
Five—Respect and admiration from the rest of the campus.
Four—Enjoy watching students cry.
Three—Never having to adapt to change.
Two—Getting to answer every question with "it depends."
And the number one reason people become financial aid administrators—What else do you do with a degree in the humanities?

Get to know this player. He or she can make the difference between winning and losing (and besides, is truly one of the nicest, most helpful people you'll meet on campus).

Chapter 5
This You Must Understand

Ubi Est Mea? (Old Latin Proverb, Translation: Where is Mine?)

THE CONCEPT OF NEED

Many high school students believe they cannot receive financial aid for an expensive private school if their parents can afford to send them to a state school. Others think that almost all financial aid is set aside for minority students. Of course, neither of these assumptions is true.

Most financial aid is based on the concept of "need." You cannot understand financial aid without understanding "need." Need should never be confused with "needy." Need is a number—nothing more, nothing less. This is how to determine the need number:

Visualize three bars, Bar A, Bar B and Bar C.

Bar A is the cost of attendance at the college of your choice.

Bar B will represent your family's expected contribution to college costs, as determined by need analysis (see previous chapter).

And Bar C is the amount of "outside" student aid you've received (e.g., private scholarships and veteran's benefits).

Bar A—the cost of attendance—is a variable. It will vary from college to college. It can even vary within one school, depending on your student status, the courses you take, how far away you live, etc.

Bar B and Bar C, which, when added together make up your contribution, are constant (unless there is a drastic change in your family's situation). It doesn't matter where you plan to buy your education. The amount you must contribute from your own resources should be the same.

If Bar A is larger than Bar B and Bar C combined, you have financial need.

Bar A—Cost of Attendance		
Bar B—Family Contribution	Bar C—Outside Aid	Need

Let's illustrate this concept of need for a family judged capable of contributing $5,000 per year to each of three colleges, College X which costs $20,000; College Y which costs $10,000; and College Z which costs $7,000.

Assuming the student has found a $2,000 scholarship, that family's need is $13,000 at College X; $3,000 at College Y; and a big fat $0 at College Z.

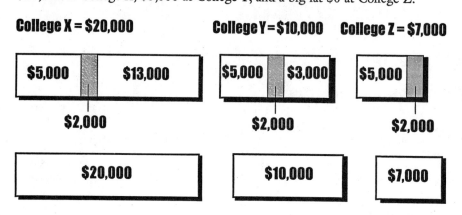

CASUAL OBSERVATION:

With a central processor and single, free application, it seems like Need Analysis should be much simpler now. It's as though Uncle Sam's plan to streamline government might finally succeed!

BEHIND THE SCENES:

Colleges that rely primarily on federal and state resources to make up financial aid packages seem satisfied with the current system of need analysis.

Students, who for the most part no longer have to pay to have their aid applications processed, seem satisfied with the current system of need analysis.

Unfortunately, colleges with a lot of institutional aid to distribute are frustrated by this simplicity. Aid administrators at these schools feel the FAFSA does not gather enough information about a family's assets to calculate a family's true ability to pay. Accordingly, many no longer use the word "need" to describe FAFSA results. Instead, they refer to the results as a "family's eligibility for federal student aid." These schools then use an application form of their own (or the College Board's PROFILE) to gather additional information and determine a student's "need" for institutional funds. More will be said about how this affects the financial aid package in Chapter 6. For now, just be warned that at many schools (especially heavily endowed, private schools), awarding aid based entirely on "need" (as determined by a uniform method of need analysis) is an ideal rather than a practice.

FINALLY:

Don't think the elements that enter into the need calculation—the family contribution and the cost of college—are carved in stone. They are elastic. They can be stretched and squeezed. This is not the time to show you how to turn rock into play-doh. But it is time to let you know it can be done. In Chapter 7 you will find a plethora of ideas for stretching and squeezing

Chapter 6
Taking Charge of the Link-Up Process

WHY TAKE CHARGE?

The admission and financial aid cycles operate on different schedules. You select colleges in the fall, apply during the winter, and get acceptance decisions in early spring. The financial aid cycle, however, cannot be formally initiated until after January first of the year in which you plan to attend college (so the computers can be fed exact data on how much your family earned the previous year). You submit your federal student aid application as soon after 1 January as possible. Then you are kept in the dark for several months before you learn (1) how much you will have to contribute, (2) whether you have need (3) whether you qualify for need-based aid (4) and what your actual financial aid package will look like. Some years, students are asked to make their decision about what college to attend before they even receive their financial aid award letter.

If you want to assume your family contribution will not cause you a cash-flow problem, and that your need will be met at whatever college you elect to attend, then you can trust the system and submit all your applications in the dark. You would be like the good soldier who carries out orders even though he does not understand them.

But if you assume, realistically, that (1) your family contribution will impose a cash-flow burden, (2) your need will not be met in all cases or (3) if it is met, it may be met in a manner that is financially burdensome to you, you cannot be a good soldier. You have to take charge of the process. In doing so, you protect your own interests. You guard against shocks and surprises. You allot adequate planning time. You improve your chances of having all your need met and met in an attractive manner. You may even succeed in lowering your family contribution and qualifying for more aid. What does all this mean? Let's translate these general statements into specifics to illustrate each point

WHAT IS MEANT BY TAKING CHARGE?

Taking charge is not complex. You won't have to enroll in a leadership or muscle-building course or graduate from Officer Candidate School. All you have to do is read this chapter and act on the advice it gives . The take-charge process has three elements:

1. **Learn the Money Numbers Ahead of Time.** Before you fill out any aid applications you should know the size of your family contribution, the costs of the colleges of your choice, and the resulting amount of need you will have at each of these schools.
2. **Execute the Application Process With Speed and Precision.** That's how you insure you'll be first in line for aid, before the "Sold Out" signs light up.
3. **Know About Influence Points.** College selection, preparing for need analysis, the speed and accuracy with which you apply, the evaluation of aid offers, financial aid administrators—these are all influence points. How you handle

Your Objective	The Good Soldier	The Take-Charge Applicant
To guard against shock.	Won't learn of family contribution until late spring. Will be surprised by amount. Has little time to raise the money and may be forced to change college plans.	Knows from the start how much college will cost family. Has almost one year to figure out how to raise money.
Make sure size of aid package corresponds to need.	When selecting colleges, does not consider their ability to meet family's need fully.	Makes schools' ability to meet need part of college selection and application strategy.
Get an attractive aid package; one that's rich in grants and low on loans.	When selecting colleges, does not consider their ability to present an attractive aid package.	Makes schools' ability to present an attractive aid package part of college selection and application strategy.

yourself as you approach these points will impact on your family contribution, aid eligibility, and size and composition of your aid award.

STEP ONE
LEARN THE MONEY NUMBERS AHEAD OF TIME

Let's begin with the first element of the take-charge process: Learn the Money Numbers Ahead of Time. You do that by securing answers to three questions:

1. How much will our family be expected to contribute to college costs? For federal aid purposes, this will be a constant. For institutional aid, it may vary.
2. What are the total costs at the college(s) of my choice? This is also a variable.
3. What's our need going to be at each college of my choice?

Once you have the answer to Question #3—even if it's just an approximation—you can begin some sensible financial planning.

QUESTION #1: HOW MUCH WILL WE HAVE TO PAY?

Family Contribution is made up of four elements: the Parents' Contribution from Income, the Parent's Contribution from Assets, the Student's Contribution from Income and the Student's Contribution from Assets (if you are an independent student, the Family Contribution will correspond to the Student's Contribution from Income and from Assets). Family contribution for the purposes of federal aid is calculated by Uncle Sam's central processor. Family contribution for the purposes of institutional aid might be calculated in a slightly different fashion, either by the College Scholarship Service or the institution itself. In other words, two different need analysis systems will be in operation for the 1997/98 school year. Both operate on the same principle. They let you shelter some of your income and assets for taxes, living expenses and retirement. Then they want whatever's left.

You should know that the income protection allowance—the money left to you for shelter, food, clothing, car operations, insurance and basic medical care—is based on the Department of Labor's "low budget standard." If you have gotten

Need Analysis System	Programs Served
Federal Methodology	1. All federal programs 2. Many state programs 3. Many collegiate programs 4. Many private donor programs
Simplified Need Test	Same as above
Institutional Methodology	1. Some state programs 2. Some collegiate programs 3. Some private donor programs

along on a low budget standard, the need analysis formula will fit you like a glove. But if you have become locked into a higher standard of living, with mortgage payments, fat utility bills, two cars, summer vacations, an occasional trip to the theater, and so on, the small allowance won't do you. It won't cover expenses. And your assessed family contribution will appear impossibly large!

The Federal Methodology is the system that will, more than any other, impact on your eligibility for student aid. It should concern you the most. Incidentally, financial aid administrators say that 95% of parents and students don't understand need analysis. Can you imagine that? Plunking down $50,000 or $100,000 for an education and not knowing how your share of that cost is assessed! You, as one of our readers, will be among the 5% who know.

The Simplified Need Test may be used by families whose total parental adjusted gross incomes (or, in the case of independent students, the student and spouse's total adjusted gross incomes) are under $50,000 and who are eligible to file a 1040EZ, a 1040A, or who do not file a tax return at all. The simplified formula is essentially the same as the Federal Methodology with the following exception: It does not count either parent or student assets in the family contribution calculation.

The Institutional Methodology is used primarily by higher priced colleges to determine eligibility for collegiate resources. The Institutional Methodology is also essentially the same as the Federal Methodology, but with a few extra questions. For example, you will have to report the value of your home.

Now it's time to calculate the family contribution under the Federal Methodology. Dependent Students go to Appendix 1. Independent Students go to Appendix 2 or 3. Your calculations won't match to the penny what the need analysis computer will determine. But the result will be close. Here are some things to know before you start filling in the figures:

Dependent Students
- All income and tax data comes from the previous calendar year. If you start college in September 1997, the previous calendar year is 1996.
- All asset data is as of the date you submit the need analysis form.
- If your parents are divorced or separated, use the income and asset figures of the parent with whom you will live for the greater part of the twelve months prior to the date of the application.
- If your parent has remarried, you must include your stepparent's income and asset information.

Independent Student

- All income and tax data comes from the previous calendar year. If you start college in September 1997, the previous calendar year is 1996.
- All asset data is as of the date you submit the need analysis form.

Dislocated Workers

If you, one of your parents, or your spouse is a dislocated worker (Chapter 4), the financial aid administrator can make some adjustments in evaluating your expected family contribution. For example, the FAA may recalculate your EFC using expected income (1997 for the 1997/98 award year) rather than previous year income.

Institutional Methodology

The worksheets allow you to calculate your EFC under the Federal Methodology. To get an idea of what private colleges (and some out-of-state public colleges) will expect you to contribute, just add the equity in your home to the total value of your assets. Your family contribution should increase by an amount equal to about 5-6% of this equity. Also, if your parents are divorced, you should assume the private college will ask about the income of the parent whose information is not listed on the FAFSA.

If you want to prepare for the absolute worst, you should add in some other assets. For example, colleges with their own aid applications may ask for the current value of your retirement accounts (IRAs, Keoghs, 401 (k)s, single premiums) and question you about sibling assets (to make sure you're not hiding money in baby brother's bank account).

The good news is, the Institutional Methodology also gives you a couple of extra allowances against income. For example, you may rework the formula subtracting unreimbursed medical expenses that exceed 4% of your AGI and tuition expenses of up to about $6,000 for each student enrolled in private secondary schools.

Again, the Federal Methodology determines eligibility for federal aid (and most state aid). It's a strict formula with little room for negotiation. The Institutional Methodology is used by many colleges to award need-based collegiate aid. The formula is not legislated so individual discretion can be wide and the room for negotiation sometimes great (depending on the policies of the school, and the desirability of the student).

Completely confused? One counselor from New Jersey lamented, "We now have two financial aid delivery systems, one for private colleges and one for public colleges."

An Important Point

Question. Why should I calculate the family contribution myself? The high school guidance office has a computer program that will make the calculation.

Answer. By making the calculation yourself you will develop an appreciation of the formula, its components, and the weights assigned to each component. When you combine this with the "advanced information" provided in the next chapter, you will get ideas for rearranging family financial data so as to obtain the most favorable analysis possible. And that can be worth a lot of money. Also, an intimate knowledge of the formula's components will serve you well later in the cycle, if you should have to discuss your aid award, and its calculation, with a financial aid administrator.

QUESTION #2: HOW MUCH WILL COLLEGE COST?

OK. You have made an estimate of your family contribution. Now you need to know how much it will cost to attend the college of your choice. College costs and tuition are not synonymous. College costs—also known as "Cost of Attendance" or "Cost of Education" or "Student Expense Budget"—are an aggregate of six elements.

1. **Tuition and fees** are generally the same for all students.
2. **Book and supply** expenditures depend on the courses you select. You can purchase these items in the college store, in the community, or you can save some money and buy them in a used book emporium.
3. **Housing** charges may vary depending upon where you choose to live; in a dorm, off-campus in an apartment, or at home, in your old room.
4. **Meal** charges can also vary. There is one figure if you purchase a school meal plan. There is another if you plan to cook for yourself (translation: pasta, pizza, tuna, and fast food). And there is still a third figure if you're enjoying home-cooked meals—it makes no difference how much this arrangement might add to your parents' costs.
5. **Miscellaneous expenses** represent all the money you spend at places other than the college. This includes upkeep of clothing, health insurance, even a small allowance for CDs, pizzas, and an occasional night out. The personal expense category can be very flexible. If you are handicapped, for instance, or have child care bills to shoulder, this item can be set very high.
6. **Transportation**, too, is flexible. It may be based on two or three roundtrip flights between a distant campus and home or it may represent commuting expenses.

If you qualify for a student loan, the costs associated with that loan (e.g., the guarantee fee and insurance premium) will also be added to your Cost of College figure.

Expense budgets are established by the aid administrator for the different categories of students who attend a typical college. There may be a separate budget for dependent students living in the dorm, dependent students in an apartment, dependent students who live at home, independent students in each of these categories, and subcategories for single and married independent students. In addition, the aid administrator will make special allowances in the budget for the unique problems of the handicapped. For example:

Single Student, Lives at Home	$11,210
Single Student, Lives in Dorm	$14,590
Single Student, Lives in Own Apartment	$15,210
Married Student, Child Care Expenses	$20,830

Here are some points to ponder about expense budgets:
- Some items in the expense budget, such as room and board when you live at home, may not represent a special outlay for your family.
- By being frugal, your actual expenditures may be less than the college has allowed.
- If some of your college-related expenses do not appear to be accurately reflected in the expense budget, let the financial aid administrator know. Any increase in the expense budget increases your eligibility for financial aid.

You can get excellent estimates of college costs from current editions of most of the comprehensive college guides (See your guidance counselor). Of course, you will want to augment this information by writing directly to colleges and asking for their most current catalogue. Also remember, if the information you're using is for the 1996/97 year, and you aren't starting college until 1997/98, you should add 6% to the total cost figure to get a better idea of the rate you'll be paying.

To get a quick idea of the relationship between your family contribution and the cost of college, we have developed a cost-of-attendance table for different types of institutions, projected to the year 2001. We've optimistically assumed 6% annual increases. Note that in a four-year, private college, your last year could cost $4,280 more than your first.

Type of Institution	1997/98 Resident	Commuter	1998/99 Resident	Commuter	1999/2000 Resident	Commuter	2000/01 Resident	Commuter
4-Year Private	$22,390	$19,160	$23,740	$20,310	$25,160	$21,530	$26,670	$22,820
2-Year Private	14,440	11,790	15,300	12,495	16,220	13,245	17,200	14,040
4-Year Public	10,720	8,535	11,365	9,045	12,045	9,590	12,770	10,165
2-Year Public	9,025	6,730	9,565	7,130	10,140	7,560	10,750	8,015

QUESTION #3: WHAT'S MY NEED?

Now you have all the materials you need to answer the third question: How much need will I have at each college of my choice? You do that by comparing your Family Contribution, as determined from Appendix 1, 2, or 3, with the Cost of Attendance (all six elements) at each school that interests you. Remember: If you're applying to one of the wealthier private schools you should perform this comparison twice: once using the federal methodology to determine your eligibility for federal aid, and again using the institutional methodology to determine your eligibility for institutional aid.

Table of Agencies, Forms and Programs

Form	Sponsor	Purpose	
		First-Come, First-Served Programs	Programs Not Time Sensitive
Free Application for Federal Student Aid (FAFSA)	Uncle Sam	Federal Campus-Based Programs	Federal Pell Grant
Renewal FAFSA	Uncle Sam	Most State Programs	Federal Family Education Loans (Stafford and PLUS)
		Some College Programs	
Electronic FAFSA	Uncle Sam	Some Private Programs	Federal Direct Loans (Direct Stafford, Direct PLUS)
State Aid Application	Your Home State	Some State Programs	Some State Programs
Financial Aid PROFILE	College Scholarship Service (CSS)	Some College Programs Some State Programs Some Private Programs	Some College Programs Some State Programs Some Private Programs

STEP TWO
EXECUTE THE PROCESS WITH SPEED AND PRECISION

Now that you've finished the first take charge step (Learn the Money Numbers Ahead of Time), you can initiate the second element: Execute the Application Process With Speed and Precision. You submit your aid application as soon after the first of the year as possible. We say "as soon after" because a great many programs operate on a first-come, first-served basis.

WHICH FORM SHOULD YOU FILL OUT?

That's up to the colleges and your home state. Be sure to find out before New Year's Day. Here are some general guidelines: Everyone must file the Free Application for Federal Student Aid (FAFSA) to be considered for federal student assistance. In addition, some families will have to use the College Scholarship Service's Financial Aid PROFILE and/or a supplemental form from their home state to be considered for collegiate or state resources. Finally, some families will have to complete an institutional aid form and send it directly to the college they hope to attend. In other words, you may have to file one, two, three or four forms depending on the wishes of your home state and the schools to which you apply.

WHY SO MANY FORMS?

Simple. College is expensive and there's not enough financial aid for everyone, so schools have to figure out who needs money the most. When Congress reauthorized the Higher Education Act, it removed "home equity" from the need analysis calculation. Suddenly zillions more people (mostly middle class people) became eligible for aid. Unfortunately, Congress did not appropriate more money to cover its largess so aid administrators had to tell families, "Sorry, I know you qualify for aid, but we don't have any money to give you." Their solution: (1) Use FAFSA results to award federal aid to all who qualify; (2) Use PROFILE and institutional aid application results to find out more about a family's finances; (3) adjust the family contribution accordingly; (4) award collegiate resources to the still needy; and (5) suggest politely that everyone else borrow more money.

Students applying to in-state schools will frequently get by with filing just the FAFSA. Students applying to more expensive schools where federal and state aid doesn't cover the tuition bill (e.g., private schools and out-of-state public schools) will usually have to complete multiple forms, as described above. *The Table of Agencies, Forms and Programs* (previous page) lists the most widely used applications and the programs they serve (including which are first-come, first served).

WHERE DO YOU GET THE FORMS AND WHAT DO YOU DO WITH THEM?

Paper FAFSAs come from your guidance office or college financial aid office. You fill it out as soon after January 1 as possible and snail mail it to the regional processor listed on the form. You pay no fee.

Electronic FAFSAs may be filed directly with the central processor using FAFSA Express. Students will find FAFSA Express at selected schools and libraries, or they may download their own copy from Uncle Sam's Office of Postsecondary Education web site (http://www.ed.gov/offices/OPE/express.html). The screen resembles the paper FAFSA and includes on-line help and instructions.

Internal edits help prevent errors and reduce rejections. Students using FAFSA Express still have to print the signature and certification page, sign it, and mail it to their regional processor (who will in turn send a signature "flag" to the central processor), but everything else may be sent electronically.

If possible, try to file electronically! Last year, processor snafus led to huge backlogs of paper aid applications and made it impossible for aid administrators to build timely financial aid packages. Electronic filers experienced none of these problems, however, they accounted for only 8,000 of the 4.8 million FAFSAs.

State aid applications (if you need one), come either from your home state (see Chapter 11) or your guidance office. Again, you fill it out (usually after January 1) and send it to the address listed on the form. You pay no fee.

PROFILE registration booklets will be in your guidance office this September. If any of your schools are listed in the registration booklet, complete the enclosed registration form and return it to CSS via mail or fax. For an extra $10, you may also call CSS (609/771-7735) and give the information to a customer service representative. You may also register electronically by visiting http://www.collegeboard.org/css/html/proform.html. CSS then sends you a packet of forms, customized with each school's financial aid questions. The basic PROFILE is nearly identical to the old FAF, but CSS has accumulated a batch of nearly 200 additional questions that schools may also choose to ask you. These questions pry into everything from the student's intended career objective, to whether the student has applied for any outside scholarships, to whether any income generating assets have recently been sold (and the purpose for which they were sold), to the year, make and model of all the family's motor vehicles. You pay a fee for all this fun; $5 just to register, then $14.50 per school.

PROFILEs may be filed prior to January 1 enabling financial aid administrators to get a head start on estimating financial aid packages. Check your schools' filing deadlines carefully.

Renewal FAFSAs will come in the mail beginning mid-November, to students who filed a FAFSA during the 1996/97 award year. Renewal FAFSAs are pre-printed with much of the data you provided last year, so unless there's a change in information, you can skip over many of the questions. If you are using the renewal application be certain to check the names (and codes) of the colleges and state agencies that are to receive the results of your needs analysis. Uncle Sam noted that last year many students neglected to do this, then wondered why the financial aid office never got a copy of their processed forms.

AVOID MAKING MISTAKES

Over 1.6 million students filed correction applications last year, listing new information or fixing errors. By filing a mistake-free form, you can be ahead of all those people in the chow line.

- **Name, Rank and Serial Number.** You must have a social security number to apply for financial aid. Furthermore, the Department of Education now verifies every applicant's name, social security and date of birth with the Social Security Administration. To minimize problems, avoid using nicknames. The computer doesn't know whether "Bill Reese" and "William Reese, Jr." are the same person. Married or divorced students must be especially careful as their last names may have changed, while their social security numbers have not.

- **January 1.** FAFSAs cannot be dated or submitted before January 1.
- **Date Due.** Be sure you know when colleges want you to submit the forms. If you apply to six colleges and each has a different deadline, submit the forms in time to meet the earliest deadline. Both FAFSA and PROFILE, remember, go to the colleges via a middleman, so you should start the process four to six weeks before your due dates.
- **Use the Right Forms.** In trying to simplify the aid process by standardizing the application, Uncle has made things more complex for some students who must now file a FAFSA as well as use PROFILE. Read each school's financial aid literature closely to make sure you know which forms to file.
- **Identify Your College Completely.** 8,200 schools participate in Uncle Sam's student aid programs. If Uncle included an institutional code list with each FAFSA packet, he would have no money left to fund aid programs, so it's your responsibility to list schools correctly—this means you must record the full name and complete address of every school that should receive your financial aid information. Remember "U. of M." could mean Maryland or Michigan. "University of California" could mean the campus at Davis or Irvine.
- **Estimating Information.** If the earliest filing date falls before your mom and dad have done their income taxes, you can use income and tax estimates on the FAFSA. If you note, later on, that your estimates were incorrect, you'll have to provide corrections. Estimators are also the most likely candidates for verification (see below).
- **Comparison Between Need Analysis Forms and IRS Forms.** College financial aid administrators verify about 30% of all financial aid forms. That's when you get to produce copies of tax forms and other documents for a comparison check. Most FAFSAs are selected based on "preestablished criteria," which is bureaucratese for "something smells fishy." Lesson: Be accurate and honest in submitting your data. If you are outside a $400 tolerance range, and did not provide any corrections, the college will know and you will be asked to make corrections. Items on the FAFSA that must match your 1040 include adjusted gross income, income tax paid and number of exemptions. Note: Some schools ask all their students for copies of their tax returns—as a matter of policy.
- **A Good Use of the Winter Holiday.** On a quiet day, switch off the TV, sit down with your family, an income tax form and a financial aid application, and put red circles around the common items. At that time, you may wish to complete the tax return so you can get a headstart on filling out the FAFSA. Remind mom and dad that the FAFSA asks whether the aid application was filled out using estimated data or a completed 1040 (which is not the same as a filed 1040). If you're going to owe taxes, you can let your 1040 sit around until April 15th, but get it filled out ASAP!
- **Be Consistent.** The FAFSA processor is programmed to crosscheck data and flag questionable applications for verification. *Example One*: A dependent student claims a one-parent family but records income for two parents. *Example Two*: A family shows $100,000 in savings, but no unearned income. Conversely, a family shows $10,000 in unearned income, but has no assets. There should be some correlation between the value of your savings and investments and the amount of your unearned income. Otherwise, lights will flash, bells will sound, and investment advice will come pouring in (or, you'll be asked to share your investment secrets). In either case, you're a candidate for verification.

- **Change in Status.** If, after you submit your FAFSA, there is a change in your status (a family death, disability, prolonged unemployment, divorce or separation), notify the college immediately. Financial aid administrators cannot make direct changes to your EFC, however, they can adjust individual data elements (e.g., lower your reportable income or assets) to reflect your new situation.

- **Early Bird Gets the Worm.** Apply for financial assistance as early as possible. Schools can often meet the needs of the first applicants, and then run out of assistance money for the late applicants.

- **Don't Make Mistakes** when filling out your aid applications. Mistakes cause the form to bounce. By the time you make corrections and resubmit it, you will find yourself at the end of the line and the money gone. Most common mistakes: Omitting social security number, recording an incorrect social security number, leaving questions blank when you mean zero, (write "0"), using "white-out," entering a range of figures such as $200-400, giving monthly instead of yearly amounts or vice versa (read each question carefully to learn what information is required), entering cents, leaving off numbers ($5,000 vs. $50,000), writing illegibly, and writing in the margins.

- **Don't forget to sign the form.** The FAFSA now includes the Statement of Educational Purpose in which you promise to use your student aid for XYZ College only. Whether you file a paper FAFSA or use an electronic version, you must sign a hard copy of this form before Uncle will authorize any funds.

- **Don't Falsify Anything.** As the top of the FAFSA clearly states, "If you purposely give false or misleading information on this form, you may be fined $10,000, sent to prison or both." And don't expect the financial planner you hired to bail you out.

- **Make Copies** of all financial aid forms and your responses to any information requests that may come from Uncle Sam, the need analysis processor or the colleges. Make sure to send the original, however, and keep the copy for yourself.

- **If You are Male (between 18 and 25), Register for Selective Service.** You will not be eligible for financial aid unless you do. If you are exempt from registering for the draft, you must file a statement accordingly.

- **If necessary, include the processing fee.** The FAFSA is free, but PROFILE costs $5 to register and $14.50 for each school that is to receive a report! (This cost is a big reason to make sure you don't waste your time on PROFILE unless your college asks you to!)

- **Finally, if you have suggestions on ways to improve the FAFSA, send them to Uncle Sam.** Every fall, an "Invitation to Comment" appears in the Federal Register. Comments about the form's design and clarity of instructions must be received by the Department of Education (Applicant Systems Division) by mid-December.

WHAT HAPPENS NOW?

The FAFSA

Your FAFSA is sent to an application processor. The processor scans in your data (or keys it in, if necessary) and transmits it to a central processor which will then convert your information into an Expected Family Contribution (EFC). A summary of all this information is sent to you. When you receive this Student Aid

Report (SAR), review it carefully to make certain your EFC was calculated using the accurate information. Also take a look at your EFC. If there's an "*" next to it, you've been selected as a candidate for verification. If there's a "C" next to it, you're a big winner—the central processor has identified an eligibility problem which must be resolved before you receive any student aid at all. The processor sends a more detailed analysis (called an Institutional Student Information Record, or ISIR) to all the colleges you named.

PROFILE

PROFILE goes back to the College Scholarship Service for processing. For yet another fee ($5.50) CSS will send a Data Confirmation Report along with your Acknowledgment. This Report shows what information CSS entered from your application and whether CSS found any problems with the way you completed PROFILE. If you see a mistake, CSS says it will correct it at no charge. Otherwise, if you need to change or update any information, you should send this new data directly to your school.

THE FINANCIAL AID PACKAGE

The financial aid administrator (FAA) now rolls up his or her sleeves and goes to work. First, the FAA determines your cost of attendance (or student expense budget). Second, the FAA reviews your expected family contribution, compares it your cost of attendance, and establishes your need (and eligibility) for most state and federal programs. Third, the FAA takes another look at your EFC to determine your eligibility for collegiate awards—about 35% of all FAAs will adjust the contribution based on policies of their office. And finally, the FAA builds your Financial Aid Package.

Before they build any aid packages, however, the financial aid staff will sit down and establish a packaging philosophy—a set of guidelines to ensure consistency and equity in their treatment of all aid applicants. Unfortunately (and ironically), each school has its own ideas about consistency and equity which means your need will probably be met differently at each school to which you apply. For example, some schools award every student the maximum Stafford possible. Others award grant aid first, then self-help (loans and work). Some have rules prescribing the ratio of grants to loans, a ratio that can vary with the income of the aid applicant (lower income students receiving more grants than loans, upper income students receiving mostly loans). Even if they don't state their packaging philosophy in their aid literature (few schools do), many schools will present you with case studies showing aid combinations for families at different income levels which can tell you everything you need to know!

In general, when awarding money from programs they administer but do not fund (i.e., federal programs), colleges tend to give priority to the neediest of the able. When awarding money from their own funds, colleges tend to give priority to the ablest of the needy.

Layer One—Pell and State Grants

The Pell Grant is the foundation of every aid package (see Chapter 10). Only students with EFCs under about $2,300 are eligible for Pells. State grants make up the other part of Layer One. Most states require students to attend an in-state college to qualify for a state award.

Layer Two—Outside Scholarships

Next, the aid administrator gleefully incorporates any outside scholarships you may have found (that's money the school need not worry about providing you). This includes the $500 awarded you by your church or temple, as well as the $5,000 from your parent's boss.

Layer Three—Federal Programs

Third, if you still have need (i.e., if the cost of college exceeds your EFC plus your Pell Grant plus your state grant plus your outside scholarships) then the FAA draws on four other federal programs: Stafford Loans, Perkins Loans, Supplemental Educational Opportunity Grants, and Work-Study (For programs specifics, see Chapter 10). The way FAAs use these programs varies from school to school according to their packaging philosophy and the size of their student aid budget. In addition to the considerations described earlier, some have policies in which they first award Stafford loans (which are limitless), preserving (scarcer) federal resources for students who then still have need. Others (primarily the less expensive schools) do the reverse, using Stafford money as a last resort.

Layer Four—Collegiate Resources

If the cost of college is still greater than all of your resources (your EFC plus money from all the aid programs just mentioned), the FAA can do one of three things:

1. Give you a huge award from the college's own resources. These resources include low interest loans and collegiate scholarships. The richer the college, the more resources it will have for this layer of the package.
2. Use the information you provided via PROFILE or the school's own aid application (i.e., the Institutional Methodology) to adjust your family contribution and if you still have need, give you funds from the college's own resources.
3. Apologize for not being able to meet your financial need fully and suggest your parents borrow money under Uncle Sam's PLUS program (or use a commercial loan source) to help ease any cash flow problems.

Layer Five—PLUS Loans

Finally, the aid administrator will approve you for a PLUS loan. The size of your loan is limited to the total program cost less any financial aid you may have received. In other words, if school costs $10,000 and you receive $5,000 in financial aid, you may receive a PLUS loan of $5,000. The size of your family contribution does not matter so long as your parents are credit worthy. For more on PLUS loans, see Chapter 10.

Families Without Financial Need

If the family has no financial need and the school really wants the student, the FAA may offer the student a non-need based award such as an academic scholarship.

THE AWARD LETTER

The FAA will present your aid package in the form of an award letter. These letters vary in format, but they all contain the following items:

1. A statement of the expense budget developed for you. Again, this varies based on factors like whether you plan to live on- or off-campus.
2. Your expected family contribution, as calculated under the federal methodology and the institutional methodology.

3. The amount of your need.
4. A description of how all or part of that need is to be met, listing each aid source and dollar amount.
4. A suspense date by when you must return the award letter.
5. Information on available procedures for "appealing" any information in the award letter with which you disagree.

If there is something you don't understand about the offer, or if you notice your EFC is different than what was sent to you by the processor on your Student Aid Report, ask the school for clarification.

Comparing Your Award Letters

While it's seldom wise to make the agonizing, final decision concerning which college to attend based on money issues alone, it's no longer realistic to exclude money as a factor (unless your family is very wealthy, in which case, why are you reading this book?). That said, it's important to make sure you're not just looking at the schools' sticker prices (that would be like comparing apples and oranges). Instead, you have to evaluate how much each school is going to cost your family in out-of-pocket money. And to make certain you're not then comparing Granny Smiths with Red Delicious, be sure to factor in the amount of loan money you'll eventually have to repay. You might find it helpful to create a worksheet (either on paper or a spreadsheet) with a side-by-side comparison of each school's package.

Compare the award letters from all the colleges to which you applied. But don't delay responding to an award letter because you are still waiting for letters from other colleges. If you don't reply by the required date, your award will be cancelled and the money freed up for some other deserving student. (Colleges can't hold money). Responding to the award letter does not commit you to attendance. It just safeguards your award, should you elect to go to that college.

In responding to the award letter, your have four choices: You can accept the award in its entirety; accept some components of the award and reject others; reject the award entirely; or request a revision in the composition of awards (more grants, less loans).

Appealing Your Award

Few people still ask us if they can challenge the admission decision. Instead, everyone wants to know if they can negotiate their aid package. Our answer? An unqualified "Maybe." With college costs increasing at a faster rate than grant aid, this topic is becoming increasingly complex and sensitive. Therefore, before your bully your way into a financial aid office demanding a recount, it's important to know what actions will help (or hurt) your cause. Your success in appealing an award depends on a great number of factors:

1. *The availability of discretionary funds.* Private colleges usually have more money for scholarships than public universities. They also have greater flexibility in how they distribute their money. In any case, make your request as early as possible, because money runs out fast even at our wealthiest schools!

2. *The skill (and tact) with which you present your case.* If your family has had a recent change in situation, document the change carefully and contact the FAA. He or she cannot just change your EFC, but he or she can adjust individual data elements that go into its calculation to allow for special conditions. These are usually unpleasant things like job loss, death, disability, divorce, or unexpected or unusually high medical expenses. In these cases, the

37

FAA will probably lower the family's income figure and recalculate. You might also ask the FAA to reduce the value of reportable assets. For example, you can easily argue a recent job loss will not only affect a family's earnings, but also eat into its savings.

3. *The caliber of the student.* If the school really wants you to enroll, the FAA can sometimes be of more help, usually by adjusting the composition of your aid package. Remember: Grants are infinitely more desirable than loans. Here's also where the line between "financial aid" and "enrollment management" can begin to blur: Informal studies show it takes about $10,000 (spread out over four years) to nab a student who might otherwise not consider a particular school. Are you the kind of student on the college's shopping list?

WILL THE NEED-BASED ROUTE SATISFY MY NEED?

Maybe. Maybe not. If it does, it could be a dream package. But, it could also be an offer that leaves you a thousand dollars short or mired deeply in debt. Remember:

- The college may not have enough resources to help all applicants.
- Different colleges may assess your need differently. If you apply to three schools, each of which costs $8,000 more than your family's EFC, you may be offered three very different packages, ranging from the attractive to the unacceptable.

STEP THREE
KNOWING THE INFLUENCE POINTS

Now that you've mastered the mechanics of need analysis, it's time for the third element of the take-charge process: Knowing the influence points.

Influence Point: Wise college selection
What You Can Gain: Improved financial aid package; no-need scholarships
More Information: Chapter 9

Influence Point: Careful preparation for need-analysis
What You Can Gain: A lowered family contribution and increased eligibility for aid; Longer planning time for help with cash-flow requirements
More Information: This chapter, Chapter 7, Appendices 1, 2 and 3

Influence Point: Speed and accuracy in applying
What You Can Gain: Increased chance of tapping into limited aid sources; Improved financial aid package.
More Information: This chapter

Influence Point: Working with financial aid administrators
What You Can Gain: Improved financial aid package.
More Information: This chapter, Chapter 7, Chapter 9

A Final Word to the Wise. There is more money in being an informed consumer and taking charge of the aid link-up process than in all the scholarship hunts ever conducted!

Part III
Advanced Moves in Financial Aid

Chapter 7
For the Short Range: Tilting Things Your Way

TILTING THINGS YOUR WAY
There are six strategies for tilting the financial aid process in your favor:
1—Reduce the Family Contribution
2—Increase the Cost of Attendance
3—Obtain an Improved Aid Package
4—Replace Your Money with OPM (Other People's Money)
5—Lower the Cost of College
6—Improve your Cash Flow

Only two of these are mutually exclusive. The Napoleon of aid seekers would probably investigate all six.

STRATEGY 1—REDUCE THE FAMILY CONTRIBUTION
Objective: Reduce your family contribution so your need becomes larger. In other words, make yourself eligible for more student assistance. We offer this advice with the hope you'll be able to distinguish between working with the system and cheating it. There's a fine line between getting your fair share, and abusing financial aid rules at the expense of needier students. Many schools have fixed (small) amounts of aid to distribute, so increasing one student's award is only possible by decreasing another's. Also remember, most aid is "need-based," not "want-based." That said, here are some ideas to ponder.

Thoroughly Understand Need Analysis
We assume that while reading Chapter 6 you took the time to complete the worksheets in Appendix 1, 2, or 3 and noted the various factors considered, including the percentages and weights assigned to your data. These are the items that should have caught your eye.

1. **Asset Assessment Rates.** A dependent student does not rate an asset protection allowance. The dependent student's assets are taxed at 35% of their value. Parents do rate an asset protection allowance. Money held by parents, as you trace it through the formula, is taxed about 5.6%. That's quite a difference! $35,000 in junior's bank account becomes a $12,250 contribution to college costs. The same $35,000 in the parental account becomes a mere $1,960 contribution. Lesson: Accumulate money for college, yes. But don't be so quick to accumulate in the child's name.

2. **The True Value of a Student Aid Dollar.** If you are in a 28% tax bracket and don't get student aid, you must earn $1.39 to have one dollar available for tuition bills. Let's turn this around. If you are successful in getting one dollar of student aid, that one dollar is really worth $1.39 to you. Lesson: The higher your tax bracket, the greater the value of any student aid dollar received.

3. **The Previous Year Rule.** Your 1996 earnings determine your aid eligibility for the 1997/98 academic year. Your 1997 earnings impact on the 1998/99

year. If your income fluctuates, and you have control over the fluctuations, you might defer income from the base year to the next. That would enhance your eligibility in the coming academic year. What about the next base year? Life is filled with soap opera twists (and the whole higher education act is up for reauthorization in 1997/98). Take it one year at a time.

4. **Business Property.** Assets that are part of a business rate an adjustment factor (e.g., 40% of net worth up to $85,000). Think hard. Do you have any source of income, from a hobby or property or whatever, that you can turn into a business? Or can you shift assets to a sub-S corporation in which your family holds a controlling 51% interest while people outside the need analysis formula (your grandmother?) hold 49%? That's a real one-two punch. Not only do you get the asset value reduced by the net worth adjustment, but there is a second reduction stemming from the 49% value transfer outside the immediate family. All this will make your tax return more complex, but the trade-off is a sharply reduced contribution to college costs.

5. **Consumer Debt.** Under need analysis, you get no write off for consumer debt. If you owe the bank $20,000 in car payments, that's your problem. But let's say you own stocks and have a brokerage account that lets you borrow against your portfolio. If you draw $20,000 from this account to finish paying for the car, you reduce the value of your reportable assets by that amount. You pay less for college and have a new car to drive!

Reduce the Value of Assets you Report for Need Analysis

Parental assets count less than student assets. Business assets count less than personal assets. But there is more.

1. Home equity is not a reportable asset under the Federal Methodology. So what happens if you use savings to pay down your home mortgage? You'll probably be in a much better position to qualify for a low-interest federal loan! (although aid administrators are free to ask questions about home equity, and may reserve the school's own funds for renters (and expect families with pricey homes and no mortgage to borrow against this great asset).

2. Do you need to make a large purchase before you sign and date your FAFSA? We've already suggested buying a car. How about a new stereo, refrigerator or washer-dryer? Pay cash, if you can. That will reduce your reportable assets— and provide you with good music, some cold drinks and a few clean clothes.

3. If you've been saving in your child's name, get his or her permission to use that money to pay your entire EFC for the first year of college. (You could also use the money for something smaller, like the increasingly essential personal computer). This will improve your chances for aid during years two, three, and four. Warning: This won't work at all schools. One of the Ivy's, for example, expects 35% of a student's assets in Year One, 35% of the remaining balance in Year Two, etc. Tricky, tricky, tricky!

Declare Yourself Independent

Independent students do not include their parents' income and assets in their need analysis calculation; only their own, (generally) more limited resources. Hence, their contribution will usually be smaller, and their need larger. Should you try to declare yourself independent then, to gain access to more aid? Certainly, if you are really independent and can convince the financial aid administrator accordingly. Absolutely not, if it is a ploy. Please note: Single, undergraduate students under the age of 24 are considered "dependent" in all cases, except at the discretion of the financial aid administrator.

Use a More Favorable Need Analysis Method

Families with adjusted gross incomes under $50,000 who are eligible to file a 1040A or 1040EZ (even if they actually file a regular 1040) may use the Simplified Methodology to calculate family contribution. In other words, parent and student assets are not considered for need analysis. If you are eligible to file a 1040A or 1040EZ and can keep your AGI under $50,000, do so!

Reduce Your Reportable Income

1. *Take less pay.* Is there any way to defer year-end bonuses? Remember, need analysis looks at previous year income—1996 for the 1997/98 award year. As Uncle Sam monitors the impact of the Higher Education Act on the federal budget and on middle income families, who knows what program adjustments he'll make in. With constantly changing rules, if you can increase your eligibility even for a year, do it!

2. *Accelerate Income.* If your student won't start college until 1998, think of ways to lower your 1997 income. For example, accelerate bonuses into 1996 and make certain you don't receive any 1996 state or local tax refunds in 1997.

3. *Accelerate or postpone gains.* If you plan to sell stocks or property, do it two years before college, or wait until your student has graduated. Capital gains count as income which is heavily "taxed" by the need analysis system. Also, watch out for year-end dividends on mutual funds. If the fund you're eying is about to pay a dividend, wait until after the payout before you buy. You'll get more shares for your money, and not have any capital gain dividends to report (per-share price drops by the amount paid out).

Start a Family Business

It doesn't have to be complex, but it does have to show a profit (in at least 3 out of 5 years, otherwise the IRS calls it a hobby). Some examples. The Bakers started Babycakes, Inc. to sell muffins every Saturday morning at their local farmer's market. Rose loved going to yard sales on weekends, so, she started a second hand furniture business with the objects she found. Uncle Sam rewards private enterprise with a greatly reduced expected contribution to college costs. Also remember, any money you pay your children becomes a business expense, and under the Federal Methodology, students receive an income protection allowance of $1,750.

Save for Retirement

Need analysis wants to know how much you contribute to a retirement fund the year before college (it considers this contribution a discretionary item and adds it back in to your total income). It does not, however, ask how much you've already saved. In other words, you can accumulate money tax-free (or tax-deferred) at the same time you reduce your assets for need analysis and save for your retirement. Please note, however, that some colleges will ask about the value of your retirement funds and either ask you to borrow against them, or use that information "against" you if try to negotiate your aid package. Also, you don't want all your assets tied up in funds that penalize you for early withdrawal (e.g., before age 59 1/2). You may need some money sooner.

Extraordinary Expenses

Does your family have enormous medical expenses? Does your family pay private secondary school tuitions for younger siblings? Were your parents divorced or separated after you filed your aid application? Was your home affected by earthquakes? Floods? The Federal Methodology no longer includes allowances for unreimbursed medical expenses, secondary tuition paid, or unpleasant events like the ones just mentioned, but leaves consideration of these special conditions to the discretion of the financial aid administrator. Make certain to let the FAA know!

Go Complex—Consult an Expert

Since you're bright, dedicated and diligent (after all, you're reading this book) you may wonder why you need additional advice. Here's the answer: College is one of the three biggest investments of your life (retirement and home ownership being the other two), yet many middle-income families fail to treat it that way!

Financial planners who really understands financial aid (and such planners are not easy to find) can help you in important ways. They'll help you understand the long- and short-term financial impact of different cost-saving strategies. They'll give you insight into how a particular school will view your case. They may even help you draft a Letter of Special Circumstance to highlight your unique situation to the financial aid office. Finally, they'll work with you on cash flow management so you can educate your children and still have enough for retirement.

Financial planners come in different flavors. You might prefer a "fee-only" planner who has no vested interest in selling you a particular investment product. Here are some cost-lowering ideas from Bonnie Hepburn, a Certified Financial Planner with MONEYSENSE Financial Planning, a fee-only practice with college funding expertise (292 Great Road, Acton MA 01720, 508/264-4088).

"Colleges claim to award financial aid consistently and objectively, but most weigh both qualitative and quantitative factors. The more the school wants a student, the more likely it is to view special circumstances favorably. Highlight those special circumstances! Special circumstances, not middle-class whining, that's the key here. If money is short because the parent took a leave of absence from work to care for an ailing relative, let the colleges know. If the parent just spent $12,000 on a wedding for an older sibling, don't mention it.

"The more persistent a parent is, *without being a nudge,* the more likely aid is. I counsel parents with endearing personalities to make personal pleas for more aid; others, I suggest send letters. One Boston parent, who was having difficulty connecting with the right person on the telephone, recently flew to Atlanta to make his case. The investment in the plane ticket payed off with $7,000 more aid per year.

"The single most important step in qualifying for aid comes in the fall when your student selects colleges to which to apply. Choose schools that compete directly with each other for students. If she applies to Washington U. in St., Louis, for example, she should also apply to Brandeis, in Boston. When the financial aid awards are made in April, be prepared to go back and negotiate, even two or three times. There are still more seats than students, and colleges would rather have a partial payer than an empty dorm space. Since negotiating with leverage is such an important part of the strategy, if you do need large amounts of financial aid, steer your student away from applying Early Decision.

"The Federal Methodology calculates Family Contribution based on income and assets. What really influences what you can afford, though, is cash flow. My advice is to work your problems from a cash flow point of view, but highlight special circumstances to the college in terms of income and assets. Here's an example.

"Jameson's parents came to me early in his sophomore year of high school (private colleges now look at two years of back tax information). Because they'd worked diligently to pay off their mortgage in preparation for college, they had a large amount of home equity. The parents had solid income ($65K), wonderful credit and the ability to borrow further against home equity. Sounds good, eh?

43

"Based on the Alice-in-Wonderland logic of aid methodology, though, it turned out not to be, because Jameson was headed for a private college and most private colleges include home equity in determining the parents' contribution. Although it didn't apply to Jameson, a new trend among private colleges is to limit countable home equity to three times income.

"Using national real estate appreciation figures from the federal government, we reduced the reportable value of the house. The parents then borrowed the remaining countable part of home equity, their intention being to convert it to a non-countable asset. Many colleges do not count assets in retirement programs, life insurance programs or illiquid investments. We chose an after-tax retirement plan.

"The Family Contribution had diminished on paper, but the family still had to make not only college payments, but also increased mortgage payments. Delighted as Jameson's parents were with the $8,000 or so reduction in college costs per year, they still needed cash flow to meet their financial obligations. Next we calculated how much his parents would need each year, and they funded an annuity accordingly.

"Here's how the immediate annuity worked. A tax loophole, testimony to the strength of the insurance lobby in America, helped them out: It's possible to withdraw money from an annuity before age 59 1/2 with no IRS penalties if you take the money out in equal payments over five years or more. (Check with your planner or tax practitioner on other age-related details.) An additional benefit of the immediate annuity approach is that only a very small amount of the withdrawal each year is taxable, since the money was taxed before it entered the program.

"Jameson's parents still had some money remaining from the refinance. They invested that money in a variable annuity, a mutual fund with a retirement wrapper. It earned money for retirement at attractive rates, tax-deferred, all the time Jameson and his siblings were in college.

"What's important here, though, is how we presented the situation to the college. We didn't talk cash flow. It makes no sense, but my experience is that cash flow arguments don't really work. What we highlighted to the college was the non-availability of home equity and his parents' inability to borrow further against nonexistent home equity. We backed this up with a letter from the bank.

"Financial planners can save you money but they can't work miracles. What they can do is help you reduce your cost of college, if possible, then help you figure out how to pay for what remains over the number of years you'll have kids in college."

STRATEGY 2—INCREASE THE COST OF ATTENDANCE
Objective: Increase the cost of attendance so your need becomes larger. This technique is most appropriate for improving your chances for a Stafford Loan.

Don't Rule Out More Expensive Schools
Your EFC is $9,000 and you plan to attend a $10,000 school. The maximum (subsidized) Stafford for which you qualify is $1,000. If you now select a $11,500 school, you qualify for a $2,500 loan. Your family contribution is the same.

Are All Your Expenses Reflected in the Cost of Attendance?
Does the aid administrator have a true picture of your transportation costs, special medical expenses, or other legitimate expenses that may have been over-looked by the school? Unfortunately, FAAs cannot include the cost of a new computer in your cost of attendance UNLESS the school explicitly requires all students to own one (many do)! Here, however, is a situation that can work! Your

family contribution is $5,000 and the FAA has established a $6,000 cost of attendance for you. The maximum (subsidized) Stafford Loan for which you can qualify is $1,000. You now convince the FAA your budget must include $500 for physical therapy made necessary by a recent car accident. Your budget now becomes $6,500 and you qualify for a $1,500 Stafford Loan.

Now you try one. Unbeknownst to the financial aid staff (as well as the admission committee), one incoming student is a werewolf. What will be the student's extra expenses? Bars for the windows. Dead bolt locks. Paying for roommate to stay at the Holiday Inn during every full moon. An occasional sack of Purina dog chow. Flea collars. Rabies shots. City dog tags. A monthly shampoo and pedicure. You complete the list...

STRATEGY 3—OBTAIN AN IMPROVED AID PACKAGE

Your aid package is loaded with loan money that, one day, you will have to repay. You don't like that. **Objective:** Change the composition of the aid package to emphasize aid that does not have to be repaid—grants and work-study.

Careful College Application

In applying to colleges, do so as early as possible, before the money runs out. Also, pick colleges where you are in the top 25% of the applicant pool. The most desirable applicants get the most agreeable aid packages. That's as true at the Ivies as it is at Horned Toad State.

Negotiate with the Financial Aid Administrator

This works only if the college really wants you. What gives you bargaining strength? Good grades and SATs, athletic ability, artistic talents, alumni ties, ethnic background, geographic origin, even a substantial financial aid package from one of the school's "competitors." Colleges like to brag about the diversity of the student body and they might be missing a pole vaulter from Idaho or a soprano from Rhode Island. Colleges also know they are competing for warm bodies. You might even ask a department head (if you are a genius) or a coach (if you are a jock) to be your advocate in such negotiations. Why do colleges care so much about all this? Long term survival! First of all, a diverse student body makes for a more rewarding academic experience for all enrolled students, but also, having an enthusiastic, diverse group of alumni spread out over the entire country is a good way for a college to ensure a continued stream of applicants in future years.

STRATEGY 4—REPLACE YOUR MONEY WITH OPM

Objective: Getting Other People's Money (OPM) to pay for your family contribution is the most desirable but also the most difficult strategy. *The Wall Street Journal* tells the story of an enterprising, financially strapped economics student who staged a one-person bike-a-thon to benefit himself. Unfortunately, pledges to his scholarship fund ($725) barely covered his expenses ($510), and after biking nearly 200 miles, alone and in the dark, he offered these words of wisdom, "stupid idea, stupid idea, stupid idea." Here are some better ones.

Money from Grandma

Direct payments to the school for tuition are not subject to the $10,000 gift tax limits, so grandparents who want to help their smart grandchildren can help pay the college bill, without having that generosity affect the financial aid calculation or anyone's tax return. No fuss. No muss.

Money from Your Boss

Many employers will reimburse you for part of your tuition expenses. See Chapter 12 for more information.

No-Need Awards

No-need awards are scholarships given with no regard to your financial need. If you win a $2,000, no-need scholarship, you are $2,000 ahead. The recipient of a no-need scholarship can fall into one of two categories with regard to college costs: They either have need or they don't. Let's examine each situation in more detail:

Situation 1—You have need and receive a no-need award

The cost of college is reduced by the amount of your award. This reduction may eliminate (1) part of your need; (2) your entire need; or (3) your entire need and part of your family contribution. Actual numbers will determine which of these it will be. Assume the cost of college is $12,000 and your family contribution is $7,000. This makes your need $5,000.

Example 1—Your no-need award is $1,000. Offered aid package: Your need is reduced from $5,000 to $4,000; your family contribution remains at $7,000.

Example 2—Your no-need award is $5,000. Offered aid package: Your need is wiped out; your family contribution remains $7,000.

Example 3—Your no-need award is $6,000. Offered aid package: Your need is wiped out; this time your family contribution is reduced from $7,000 to $6,000.

This packaging may seem unfair, but colleges have very little choice about how they use your no-need award—federal regulations require them to include the money as part of your family's expected resources for college before they can use it to replace any of your EFC. In Examples 1 and 2 above, students can still benefit greatly from the no-need award by convincing the FAA to use the money to replace a loan element of their aid package.

Situation 2—You have no need and the award is a no-need award

In this case, the money goes directly to you. It replaces your money. You write a smaller check when you pay the college bill. Let's assign numbers to this. Your family contribution is $9,000 and the cost of college is $9,000.

Example 1—Your no-need award is $3,000. Your family contribution shrinks to $6,000. That's all you have to pay.

Example 2—Your no-need award is $10,000. Now you're $1,000 ahead which will finance your winter tour to the Yucatan. Right? Wrong. You can only receive $9,000—the amount that eliminates your family contribution. Financial aid can't exceed the cost of attendance. In other words, it cannot provide income for you.

Where can I find no-need awards?

No-need awards tend to congregate in the following three areas.

Uncle Sam. Most of Uncle's no-need awards have a military connection and carry a service obligation, e.g., service academies and ROTC scholarships.

The States. Two types of programs. Honor scholarships for outstanding students and tuition equalization grants for in-state students who attend a private college rather than a public university. Both programs usually require students to remain in their home state. See Chapter 11 to learn whether your state operates either program.

The Colleges. Colleges are the main source of no-need awards. Most are academic scholarships designed to entice bright students to enroll at the sponsoring institution. See *The A's and B's of Academic Scholarships* (inside back cover).

STRATEGY 5—LOWER THE COST OF COLLEGE

Attempt to lower the cost of college so as to reduce or eliminate your need. **Objective:** To avoid going through the hassle of applying for aid or saddling yourself with debt following graduation.

Pick a Lower-Priced School

Choose a school in an area where the cost of living is low (e.g., Texas, Michigan) or one that receives church subsidies (e.g., Brigham Young, St. Olaf). And most importantly, don't overlook your own State U.

You might also go to a community college for two years, then transfer to a four-year school to finish your degree. You pick up the "halo" of the prestige college's sheepskin, but at a fraction of the cost.

Examine Each Element that Makes up "Cost of Attendance"

Some are firmly established (such as tuition), but you can influence others. For example, used books cost less than new ones, softcover costs less than hardcover, and many airlines have incredible student rates! (or you might use an airline's credit card to pay tuition and use the resulting frequent flier miles for free round trips to campus). Students can also save money by living off-campus with roommates, or choosing a meal plan that fits their lifestyle (don't pay for breakfast at the dining hall if you know you never wake up before noon).

One of the easiest ways to control your college costs is to stay away from credit cards. It's all too easy to run up large debts, and credit card shopping sprees are usually not for school-related essentials. It's not too soon to learn one of life's little lessons: The only way to stay out of debt is to spend less money than you have! You'll find out all about debt when you start repaying your student loans; don't add high-interest credit card debt to the mix.

Look for Other Savings

Parents may qualify for lower car insurance when their risky teenage driver heads to college. Also, keep track of pre-college costs. Campus visits, test prep courses, application fees and private counselors can cost thousands. Be judicious.

Accelerate College

Take college courses for credit while in high school or get credit on advanced placement exams. Last year, 400,000 students took 600,000 tests receiving passing scores (3, 4 or 5) on over half of them. About 1200 schools give credit for good AP scores (although many are boosting their minimum acceptable score from 3 to 4); hundreds (including Harvard) grant incoming students sophomore standing. Each credit hour you pick up can be worth as much as $400 (depending on the college's tuition costs). A test costs only about $75.

Another option is the three-year degree. High profile figures from Stanford and Oberlin have praised the idea. Others feel most students need the full four years to grow, intellectually, emotionally, and occupationally. They're afraid the liberal-arts will get short-changed as students won't have enough time to take the necessary spectrum of courses.

But whatever you do, don't take more than four years to graduate!

Investigate External Degree Programs

There are lots of ways to go to school without setting foot in a classroom. The best summary of these external degree programs is *College Degrees by Mail* by John Bear, $12.95, Ten Speed Press, PO Box 7123, Berkeley, CA 94707. For example:

1. Take correspondence courses. Regents College of New York seems the most comprehensive, offering 26 associate and baccalaureate degrees. Students may enroll at any time, and move through the program at their own pace. Regents College offers no classes of its own. Rather, it accepts a wide array of credit from accredited sources including distance instruction, campus-based courses at other colleges and universities, and special assessment. Regents College also provides enrolled students with access to its own database of over 7,000 distance learning options. Students work with an academic advisor by mail, phone, fax and e-mail to plan their course of study. Regents College serves nearly 20,000 resourceful, independent learners each year. For program information, write Regents College, The University of the State of New York, Dept. DMO, 7 Columbia Circle, Albany, NY, 12203, 518/464-8500 or visit their web site at http://www.regents.edu.

2. Get your education through public television. Many stations have agreements with colleges to offer courses for credit. Mind Extension University, in conjunction with George Washington U., Kansas State (and nine others), lets cable subscribers get course credit at home that they may later apply toward degree programs at participating colleges. Sample courses include: Analytical Geometry and Calculus, American Poetry Post-1900, Family Relationships, Conversational French, the US Constitution, and Economics (Macro- and Micro-). Call 800-777-MIND for tuition and registration information. *Warning*: Make sure you check the accreditation for these programs. Nonaccredited courses will not count toward a degree. Also, don't try to argue that a $4,000 wide screen TV should be part of your cost of college figure! This strategy won't get you far in your quest for student aid.

3. Graduate from http://www.almamater.edu. Computers, modems, phone lines and virtual universities are the next wave in external degrees. The aptly named Thomas Edison State College (Trenton, NJ), for example, has no faculty, no library, no student center, and no football team. In fact its hub is little more than a 2 foot by 3 foot Digital Equipment Corporation VAX 4000 computer. The school contracts with faculty members at nearby schools to "supervise" courses. Accepted students receive a course package that includes textbooks and videos and software for phone connections. They use electronic mail to communicate with faculty (called mentors) and other classmates, get reading assignments, and submit papers. Classroom "discussions" (via e-mail) are extensive. Only graduation still takes place on campus!

The (for-profit) University of Phoenix has started advertising its online campus quite heavily. It's fully accredited and located at http://www.uophx.edu/online.

With huge projected increases in the number of college-bound students, many states are also considering "electronic institutions" rather than expanding physical campuses. Twelve Western governors have discussed working together to create a virtual university. Florida, Iowa, Kentucky, Maine, Minnesota, New York, North Carolina, Virginia, and Wisconsin are also all in the process of introducing or expanding state networks to link students and schools.

You can also attend classes via America Online (AOL) or the Internet. It's nearly impossible to keep up with all the e-mail addresses and web sites, however students will soon have their pick of hundreds of credit and non-credit courses. For information about AOL's Electronic University Network, select EUN from AOL's education menu. Costs range from $59 to $300 per credit hour (excluding on-line time). For information about courses offered via the Global Network Academy, go to http://www.gnacademy.org. Costs range up to $100 per credit hour (again, excluding on-line time).

4. Get credit for life experience. Different schools have their own rules on what counts for what credit. The American Council on Education publishes guidelines in a book called *The National Guide to Educational Credit for Training Programs.* Another option is to take the College Board's College-Level Examination Program (CLEP) Test or the ACT's Proficiency Examination Program (PEP).

STRATEGY SIX—IMPROVE YOUR CASH FLOW

Your family contribution must be paid each semester. For those who have assembled vast quantities of worldly goods, the family contribution can represent a rather sizable sum that usually comes with a friendly note "unless this bill is paid by such and such a date your student will not be allowed to register for classes..."

How can you pay this bill without selling the family home, jeopardizing your after-retirement financial security or taking out a high-cost commercial loan? You could turn to Uncle Sam's loan programs (the Stafford and PLUS). But Uncle's loans have some drawbacks. One, they are subject to the whims of the political process. And, two, they have the usual comet's tail of paperwork, back-and-forth mailings, and other rigmarole generally attached to federal programs. **Objective:** To pay your family contribution without liquidating assets, hocking the family jewels, or playing Uncle Sam's paper games.

Choose Colleges with Innovative Payment Plans

Many colleges offer favorable, middle-income loan programs, using money either from its own endowment funds or through money raised by state tax-exempt bond issues. Other schools allow you to pay the family contribution in installments. See Chapter 9.

Participate in Commercial Tuition Payment Plans

Here is how most plans work: You determine your cash requirement for college—say $1,500 at the start of each semester. The commercial organization forwards that money to the school twice a year, then collects ten $300 payments from you spread evenly over a number of months. You pay no interest, but must start making your payments well before your tuition bill is due. Frequently, plans charge a flat $40-$50 fee and have a life insurance feature to cover bills in the event of your death. Payment plan sponsors include:

KNIGHT College Resource Group. 855 Boyleston Street, Boston, MA 02116, 800/225-6783 (or 617/267-1500)

Tuition Management Systems. 4 John Clarke Road, Newport, RI 02842, 800/ 722-4867, 401/849-1550, http://www.afford.com.

Academic Management Services. 50 Vision Blvd., East Providence, RI 02914, 800-635-0120

Education Credit Corporation, 2252 Morello Avenue, Pleasant Hill, CA 94523, 800/477-4977.

Many of these companies also sponsor commercial loans. For example, KNIGHT College Resource Group offers the Achiever Loan with an interest rate equal to the 13-week T-bill plus 4.5%. For other major loan sources, see below.

Borrow from a Commercial Loan Source

With the growing threat to interest subsidies in federal loan programs, expect these plans to multiply over the next few years. But be sure to compare plans before you sign on any dotted lines. Finance charges can vary greatly, as can the repayment schedules. Here are four of the largest commercial loan sources:

TERI offers loans of up to the total cost of education (less any financial aid received) with 20-25 years to repay. Repayment begins 45 days after loan disbursement, although families may defer paying back the principal while the student is enrolled. Families also pay a guarantee fee equal to 5% of the total loan amount. The interest rate equals the prime rate plus 1-2%. TERI also sponsors the Professional Education Plan (PEP) for graduate students. Contact The Education Resource Institute, 330 Stuart Street, Suite 500, Boston, MA 02116, 1-800-255-TERI.

NELLIE MAE. The New England Loan Marketing Association offers similar loans (EXCEL. GradEXCEL and SHARE). For more information, write Nellie Mae, 50 Braintree Hill Park, Suite 300, Braintree, MA 02184, 800-634-9308 (in MA, 617-849-1325), http://www.nelliemae.org.

SALLIE MAE. The Student Loan Marketing Association offers a wide variety of programs for both graduate and undergraduate students. Its Signature Education Loan Program combines Stafford loans with private supplemental loans, providing students and their families with a comprehensive source of education loan funding throughout the student's college career. For more information, contact SALLIE MAE, 1050 Thomas Jefferson Street, NW, Washington, DC 20007, 800-828-0290, http://www.salliemae.com.

GATE. Guaranteed Access to Education. Loan limits are set by participating schools. No origination or guarantee fees. No payments during full-time enrollment (interest, however, accrues). Repayment begins four months after graduation. Payments are interest-only for the first five years, followed by eight years of increasing payments of principal and interest. Contact GATE, 7 Tucker's Wharf, Marblehead, MA 01945, 800-895-GATE, http://www.gateloan.com.

PLATO. Loans of up to $25,000 per year with 15 years to repay. Use funds for all education-related expenses, even $3,000 for a personal computer. Repayment begins 30 days after the student receives the loan money (although families may defer repaying the principal for up to four years while the student is enrolled). Contact PLATO, 205 Van Buren St. #200, Herndon, VA 22070, 800-GO-PLATO, http://www.uss.org/plato.htm.

Tap Your Home Equity

If your family has a good credit history, you can generally borrow up to 80% of the market value of your home minus the outstanding balance of your mortgage. In other words, if you own a $100,000 home and have $30,000 left on the mortgage, you can borrow up to $50,000. Calculation: (100,000 x .8)-30,000=$50,000. You must usually pay a small fee to open an account, but after that, you can borrow whatever you need, whenever you need it, without having to reapply. To use the funds, you simply write a check or use a credit card. Interest rates float about two percentage points above the prime. And here's an added bonus. Any items you charge against your credit line—like college tuition—will become part of your home mortgage, so, your interest payments on loans up to $100,000 become tax-deductible.

Home equity loans are an extremely easy and flexible way to obtain cash flow assistance on favorable terms. In fact, they allow many families to live way beyond their means, so take care that ease of access to all this money does not result in deep financial problems and cause you to lose your home. The total monthly payments on all of your loans should not exceed 35% of your pre-tax monthly income. Also make certain you choose a line of credit over a loan. The reason? You won't need all the money at once. In fact, in between tuition bills you should pay down as much of your debt as possible, so you never use up more of your equity than necessary.

When shopping for the best deal, beware of teaser rates. They're usually only good for the first six months or a year. Here are some other questions to ask: What is the rate of interest? If it's variable, how often can the rate change? On what index is it based? Does it carry a cap? Is there an annual fee? An application fee? An origination fee? Can any of the terms change without my approval? Are there any points charged? What about closing costs? Under what circumstances can the bank require repayment of the outstanding credit?

Hold a Yard Sale

Now that Junior is heading off to school, maybe it's time to start unloading "stuff." even a modest yard sale can net $1,000.

Borrow Against Your 401(k)

If you participate in a company pension plan like a 401(k), you may be able to borrow against it. Or, if you are a self-employed professional with a retirement plan, you can do some borrowing. Under tax reform, you can borrow half the vested amount up to $50,000, less your highest loan balance during the preceding twelve months. The interest rate hovers around the prime, you pay no fees or points, and the cash is available very quickly. To avoid tax and penalties you must repay your account within five years (you have longer if the money is used to buy a home). Payments are usually made via payroll deductions. If you decide to use this option, make certain to borrow enough to cover a full year's tuition, not just a semester, since employers may impose additional regulations, such as only one loan per year. If at all possible, however, consider borrowing from some other source. Raids on your 401(k) will cause your fund to grow at a much slower pace, and if you're like most parents, you really do need this money for your retirement.

Use Your IRA

You'll probably be hit with a 10% penalty and a bill from the IRS, so, if you need $6,000, draw out a little extra to take care of both the bursar and Uncle Sam. As usual, there's an exception. This time it's found in Section 72(t)(2)(A)(iv) of the tax code (or thereabouts). You can escape the tax collector and withdraw funds before you turn 59 1/2, provided you receive the money in equal, periodic payments extending over the rest of your years. You can even modify these payments— after the later of five years or turning 59 1/2.

"WHAT IF" CALCULATIONS

Now that you've mastered the advanced course in need analysis and cash flow, you should try a few "what if" situations, using the worksheets in the Appendices. If you have a home computer with spreadsheet software, these appendices are easily programmed, and make "what-if" calculations simple. Another option is to order our software package (see inside back cover). The results can surprise you.

Here Are a Few "What-if" Suggestions

1. How does a charitable gift of $1,000 impact on your family contribution?
2. Should Mom get a job to help with college costs? Or, should Mom quit her job to increase eligibility for financial aid?
3. If Dad needs to complete his degree, is there any advantage to his returning to school at the same time one or more children are in college?
4. If you have two children, one year apart, with one starting college and one starting the senior year in high school, would it be advantageous for the older child to "stop out" for one year and wait for son or daughter #2 to catch up?

5. Do grandparents need some extra money? You can each give each of your student's grandparents a gift of up to $10,000. That could reduce your assets by as much as $80,000. It could also reduce the amount of tax being paid, as frequently, grandparents are retired and in a lower tax bracket.
6. Can you shift some assets into a business venture?
7. Can you lower your AGI to under $50,000?
8. What happens if you make a large purchase, such as a car, and pay cash or borrow against a stock portfolio?
9. What happens if you pay down your mortgage?
10. Try some "what-ifs" of your own.

WHAT PEOPLE WON'T TRY

Students buy campus property. Linda Wallace, a University of Wisconsin student, purchased a condo near the campus for $60,000. When she graduated, she sold it for a $30,000 profit—enough to pay off nearly four years of college expenses. Becky and Louis James moved to San Diego to attend the University of California. They bought a three-bedroom house and collected rent from roommates. The James' are tickled pink with their investment. The rent covers mortgage payments. And, by owning property, the James' established California residency, saving each more than $1,000 a year in out-of-state tuition. Of course, Linda and the James' also saved on college room and board charges.

Mom and Dad buy campus rental property. This takes a more sophisticated approach. Not only do you get the benefits of deducting mortgage interest, operating expenses and depreciation, but your college student offspring can receive a steady salary while in school; a salary you may deduct as a business expense. How? By having your student live in one of the units and draw pay from you as property manager. At the same time, he or she saves on room and board. In addition, your campus visits can be written off, because, as far as the tax collector is concerned, the purpose of the trip is to inspect your property. And, if your real estate appreciates, you can sell the property and pocket the after-tax share of the capital gain. There is still one more advantage. If you purchase the property with funds that used to be personal assets, and you make certain the property becomes part of a formally recognized business, you have moved them into the business category which provides you with a net worth adjustment in the need analysis formula.

To take advantage of all this, be sure your property qualifies as rental (and not personal) property. In other words, Mom or Dad cannot use it for more than 14 days or 10% of the total days they rent it out. Here's why: The IRS distinguishes between the treatment of personal property and the treatment of rental property. The IRS limits deductible losses from personal property to the amount of rental income received. The IRS places no such limit on losses from rental property, however, these losses may no longer be used to offset salary income. They may only be used to offset what the IRS calls passive income—income from limited partnerships or other rental property. Furthermore, the IRS limits the deduction of mortgage interest to the amount allocated to rental use (if, however, the property is rented for 100% of the year, 100% of the mortgage interest may be deducted). There is still some good news in all this. Families with AGIs under $100,000 who actively manage their property, may use up to $25,000 of real estate losses to shelter "nonpassive " (salary) income. NOTE: The IRS has 266 pages of rules on passive/active losses. We've tried to summarize it here, but suggest you speak with an accountant or tax attorney before you undertake this kind of venture.

Get on Mom or Dad's payroll. Can either of your parents give you a job in the family business? If so, it's a great way to shift some income! Your earnings become a tax deductible business expense. If you're under 18, you do not have to pay social security tax on your wages. And, if you can limit your earnings to under $4,000 per year ($6,000 if you contribute to an IRA), you will owe no federal income tax. Assuming you start this when you enter high school and your parents pay about 40% in federal, state and local taxes, they will receive $9,600 in deductions. Of course, under the federal methodology, schools will grab about $7,725 of the $24,600 you've earned. Calculation: 35% of all non-retirement assets (c. $16,000) plus 50% of prior year income ($6,000) over $1,750, but isn't that what the money was for anyway? Meanwhile, you're also beginning to save for retirement. Even without additional contributions, your $8,000 IRA (at 8%) will grow to nearly $335,000 by the time you're 65!

Give a gift. An individual can make a $10,000 tax-free gift each year to another individual. A married couple can double that and make it a $20,000 gift. Under conventional wisdom, grandparents are the ones who usually take advantage of this tax wrinkle to help their smart grandchildren with college. Under unconventional wisdom, (as we explained under "what-ifs" to try) parents might consider making an annual gift to grandparents. The purpose: To reduce their own asset position for need analysis and pay less for college. The money, meanwhile, really did not leave the family. A gift of securities is especially advantageous. If they have appreciated, you avoid paying tax on the gain. And, if they continue to appreciate after they have been transferred, they can be inherited at this higher value, and still no one has had to pay tax on the gain.

Start an educational benefit trust. Small, closely held corporations can establish trusts to pay the college expenses of employees' children—that means all employees—the president's as well as the staff's. The corporation makes regular payments to the trust. Once an eligible person reaches college age, a predetermined amount of tuition money is withdrawn. This disbursement must be treated as a taxable benefit by the student's parents. Thus, the president who is in a higher bracket will probably gain less than a member of the staff.

Start a company scholarship program. This is not as complex as a trust. Still, the program must meet an IRS test to qualify as a business expense. The test usually involves a set of standards. For example, beneficiaries must have a B average; their mother or father must have worked for the company at least five years. A second part of the test deals with eligibility. All employees' children must be eligible. If too many scholarships go to the children of corporate officers and directors, the company will flunk the test.

Borrow against a brokerage account. This is another way to avoid the "non-deductibility of consumer interest" feature of the tax laws. If the margin loan is used to buy investment property, interest is deductible up to the amount of investment income produced. We suggest you sell some securities to pay your college bills (maybe some whose values have dropped, to generate a loss, for tax purposes), use a margin loan to buy back the securities (if you're repurchasing securities, be careful to wait 30 days, otherwise the IRS won't let you take the loss). If you do decide to borrow against your brokerage account (this is known as a margin loan), be very careful. Borrowing limits are usually 50% of the account value. If your margined security takes a tumble on the market, your broker will require more cash or collateral to maintain your loan. Note: You can't deduct interest on a loan used to buy tax-exempt investments such as municipal bonds, because you don't pay tax on the resulting income from these bonds.

Chapter 8

Long-Range Planning: College Is Still Years Away

COLLEGE IS STILL YEARS AWAY

You've seen them. Charts that tell you to save $800 a month from now until your newborn turns 18 if you want to afford college in the year 2014 (to say nothing of the savings requirements for families with two or three children). You are best advised to ignore these charts and any other "scare-the-pants-off-you" marketing strategy employed by organizations who, of course, will be pleased to help you save (and invest) that $800 per month. Instead, you should save as much money as you can afford, do it systematically, but be realistic, and remember, when your student enters college, your savings can be supplemented by a contribution from your earnings, their earnings and a manageable loan. If you feel you absolutely must use one of those "How Much You'll Need to Save" charts—a better goal might be to save enough to cover half the cost of college (also remember, you don't have to have the entire amount saved by the time your student first enrolls. He or she will be there for at least four years...make certain this expanded time frame is reflected in the chart's numbers). Still nervous? Think about buying a $200,000 home. Do you wait until you've saved the entire $200,000? Or do you think in terms of saving enough for the downpayment?

HOW YOUR SAVINGS GROW

The chart below shows how your college fund grows if you're stashing away $100 per month. In the short run, the rate of return seems to make very little difference. Over 20 years, however, the difference between 7% and 12% comes to $47,510. Lesson: Start saving early. Take a chance on riskier investments. Let compound interest work for you. Switch to safe investments when college bills loom near.

	7%	8%	10%	12%
Year 1	1,245	1,250	1,267	1,281
Year 2	2,580	2,610	2,670	2,725
Year 3	4,020	4,080	4,215	4,350
Year 4	5,550	5,675	5,920	6,185
Year 5	7,200	7,400	7,810	8,250
Year 7	10,860	11,285	12,195	13,200
Year 10	17,410	18,415	20,655	23,235
Year 12	22,600	24,210	27,875	32,225
Year 15	31,880	34,835	41,790	50,460
Year 20	52,400	59,290	76,570	99,910

RULE OF 72

For novice investors, the Rule of 72 is a quick way to see how fast your money will grow. If you divide 72 by your investment's expected rate of return, the resulting answer is the length of time it will take for your money to double. For example, your $10,000 investment is earning 6%. In twelve years (72/6) it will be worth $20,000. At 8%, your $10,000 will equal $20,000 in just nine years.

TAX PLANNING VS. COLLEGE AID

When college is still years away, the name of the game is to accumulate enough money to help with the inevitable bills. Unfortunately, plans to minimize tax liability sometimes run counter to plans to maximize financial aid eligibility—making decisions about saving money more complex. The trick is knowing when tax planning and college planning run counter to each other, and when they are complementary.

Example 1: The first decision a family must make is whether to save money in the parents' or the child's name. For tax purposes, unearned income derived from parental assets can be assessed at a higher rate than unearned income from a child's assets. (For children under 14, the first $650 in interest or dividend income is tax-free. The next $650 is taxed at the child's rate. And any unearned income in excess of $1,300 is taxed at the parents's rate.) For financial aid purposes, however, parental assets are assessed at no more than 5.6% while student assets are assessed at a flat 35%. This often wipes out all the tax advantages previously received. The lesson? If there's any chance the family will qualify for financial aid, save in the parents's name.

Example 2: In saving for retirement, you don't pay taxes on the money you contribute to 401 (k)s, 403 (b)s, Keoghs, or SEP-IRAs. Furthermore, your money grows tax-deferred year after year. For financial aid purposes, the money you have saved in retirement accounts is excluded from need analysis, making saving for retirement one of the most effective ways to also lower your expected family contribution.

GETTING GOOD FINANCIAL ADVICE

Where do you go to get good advice on maximizing savings, both for college and for retirement? Most people can get all the information they need by clipping articles from consumer-oriented personal finance magazines like *Kiplinger's, Money, Smart Money, Worth, Fortune,* and *Forbes.* Other people rely on a stockbroker for advice about the marketplace, an accountant for tax strategies, and an attorney for the latest on trusts and estates. Between these three groups of professionals, families can get a lot of sound advice on financial planning. There is, however, an emerging group of professionals who should be able to combine the advice you get from your broker, your accountant and your lawyer—that is the certified financial planner.

Financial Planners to the Rescue

Personal finance experts appear under many guises—stockbrokers, financial planners, bankers, accountants, and insurance agents. Most of these people are bright, resourceful professionals who can be of genuine help in the college financing process. Unfortunately, some of them are good at planning only one thing—their own lucrative retirement. Before you enlist in any of their services, learn something about investing, write down your objectives, and ask questions.

Are they fee only planners or do they work on commission? About how much are you going to pay for their services? Fee only planners charge by the hour. While this may cost you more money in the short-run, fee only planners point out that their counterparts don't always have real incentives to provide you with totally unbiased service (i.e., some planners will give you nothing but a glossy sales pitch for whatever products bring the largest commission). If possible, find out how much of the planner's income comes from each of four sources: commissions, fees you pay for advice, fees you pay for them to manage your funds, and fees they receive from companies that pay them to sell their products. And don't confuse fee-only planners with fee-based planners who charge both fees AND commissions.

What are their fields of expertise? Their investment strategies? Are they selling you boilerplate from a parent company or is truly a personalized plan? Your planner should be familiar with investment strategies of all types—traditional advice on retirement planning and estate planning is not necessarily compatible with sound college planning. Your advisor should be able to explain these possible conflicts and help you maximize all of your resources (while minimizing your tax consequences). And, your planner should be a good listener, keeping your comfort level in mind while helping you with your financial plan.

What is their prior work experience? Did they get their start in law? Accounting? Insurance? A brokerage house? A college financial aid office? Charm school? How long have they been in business? How many clients do they have? How many new clients per year? Unless it's a firm specializing in short-term college planning, heavy turnover is a bad sign!

What are their professional credentials? Do they still have ties to an insurance company or brokerage house? Are they with an established company such as American Express or Waddell & Reed? Have they been certified by a reputable group such as The Institute of Certified Financial Planners?

Is the planner providing you with a service you can't get from your accountant, your stockbroker or your lawyer? There is no sense in paying for the same service twice.

Finally, ask for references. Reputable planners will be only too happy to oblige. Most will be registered with the Securities and Exchange Commission as investment advisors. You can ask the planner for a copy of the forms they filed (Form ADV), or request the information directly from the SEC (Branch of Public Reference, Office of Filings and Information Services, 450 Fifth Street, Mail Stop 1-2 NW, Washington DC, 20549, 202/942-8090, http://www.sec.gov). Include your daytime phone number, state your specific request and indicate your willingness to pay for copying and shipping, and for about a quarter a page, the SEC will tell you all about the planner's academic, professional and work history.

For more information, or to find a planner in your area:
- American Society of CLU and ChFC, 800/392-6900. Insurance agents and planners with an insurance orientation, these chartered financial consultants must also have at least three years experience in the field.
- Institute of Certified Financial Planners, 800/282-7526.
- National Association of Personal Financial Advisors, 800/366-2732. Trade group of fee-only planners.
- International Association for Financial Planning. 800/945-4237. Trade group that requires members to have a state license, or SEC registration.
- American Institute of Certified Public Accountants 800/862-4272. Personal Financial Specialists, or CPAs who have passed a financial planning test and have practical financial planning experience.

Seeing the Sites

Professional money managers no longer have the same information advantage they used to. Personal finance sites litter cyberspace, and with a few mouse clicks you can find everything from full research reports to financial news headlines to mutual fund prospectuses to ten-minute stock tickers. Investment houses (J.P. Morgan), brokerage firms (Merrill-Lynch) personal finance magazines (Money, Kiplinger's, Forbes, Fortune), and mutual fund companies (Fidelity, Vanguard) all have little treats for you.

Of course, most site sponsors give you this free information because they want you to subscribe to their publications or give them all your money to invest, but that's no reason to forsake their largess. Just be a savvy surfer. One good (less commercial) starting place is The Syndicate, http://www.moneypages.com/syndicate/index.html. Its partially-annotated links take you to stock sites, bond sites, mutual fund sites and 1,600 other finance-related sites, ranging from accounting to forecasts to newsletters to taxes. If you're primarily interested in mutual funds, try Mutual Funds Interactive, http://www.brill.com/index.html.

SAVINGS PHILOSOPHIES

Ask ten financial advisors to recommend the best way to save for college and you're likely to get ten very different answers. First, you must decide how the money should be saved—in the parents' name? the child's name? a trust? Then you must decide how much risk you're willing to take with your money.

It's very difficult to offer sound investment advice in a vacuum, i.e., without knowing how much risk a family is comfortable with taking. As a general rule, the safer the investment option, the lower the return. The riskier the option, the greater the return (as well as the potential for a huge loss). Most of the plans described in this chapter are safe, or as some would say, plain vanilla, and don't require professional fund managers to turn a profit.

How can you tell if your portfolio is too risky? If you consistently wake up in the middle of the night concerned about a price drop in your stock or bond fund, you should rethink the composition of your portfolio.

How else can you tell if an investment is right for you? If you don't understand the investment, its liquidity, its true costs, or how it works, then stay away.

SAMPLE PORTFOLIOS

The composition of your portfolio should change with the age of your children. When they are young, you can afford to take more risks than you can when tuition bills are just around the corner. Here's one example:

The Early Years (Under 6). About 90% of your money should be in stock funds, split between aggressive growth (the most risky) and growth and income (less risky). The other 10% should be in something safe like a money market or CD.

The Middle Years (6 to 13). You should keep about 90% in stock funds, but shift the money out of aggressive growth and into more conservative growth and income.

The Pre-College Years (14 to 17). According to personal finance expert Jane Bryant Quinn, money you'll need within four years shouldn't be invested in a mutual fund, because historically, that's how long it takes for stocks to drop from a peak and rise back to the original price. Our advice? During these years, aim to keep 50% of your money in a growth and income fund, and start moving the rest (over the next four years) into CDs or a money market.

If you don't think you're going to qualify for financial aid, this is also the time to consider switching money from your name into your child's. If you transfer appreciated stock funds into your child's account before you convert them into safer investments, the profit will be taxed at the child's lower rate (probably 15%), and save you thousands of dollars.

PAY YOURSELF FIRST

The best way to accumulate money is to pay yourself first, and use an investment strategy called Dollar-Cost-Averaging. The premise is simple. You have a fixed amount of money withheld from your paycheck each month and invest that money in something like a mutual fund; you don't have to worry about whether the market is up or down, and you're pretty certain to be safe from financial disaster. In fact, you'll probably do better than most professional fund managers. Why does this work? Let's say you have $200 withheld from your paycheck and wired into a brokerage account each month where it buys shares of your favorite mutual fund. When the market is up, your $200 buys relatively fewer shares than when the market is low, so the average cost of your shares is lower than the average price during the period.

	Monthly Investment	Price per Share	Shares Purchased
	$200	$25	8.00
	$200	$25	8.00
	$200	$30	6.66
	$200	$25	8.00
	$200	$20	10.00
	$200	$25	8.00
Totals	$1,200	$150	48.66

Your average cost per share is $24.66 ($1,200/48.66) while the average market price per share is $25 ($150/6). You win! Here's another way to look at your smart investment: Had you simply purchased 8 shares each month, you would have only 48 shares for your $1,200. Now you have 48.66. You win again! This method of regular, systematic savings will allow you to accumulate funds fast, especially if you start when your children are very young!

CUSTODIAL ACCOUNTS AND TRUSTS

Families that want to save money in the child's name have two main choices—custodial accounts and trusts.

Custodial Accounts under the Uniform Gift to Minors Act (UGMA) accept money. Custodial accounts under the Uniform Transfer to Minors Act (UTMA) also accept property. Both are irrevocable gifts to a child where a custodian is responsible for managing the funds until the minor reaches the age of majority. The money which accumulates does so under the minor's lower tax liability. UGMA and UTMA accounts are easy to set up (just call your banker or broker), but they have one major drawback. Once the funds are turned over (as early as age 18), the child can do whatever he or she wants with them. Pay for college, pay for a new car, pay for a lifetime supply of jelly donuts...Individuals may make a tax-free gift worth up to $10,000 to either of these two accounts

Minority Trust. Under section 2503(c) of the tax code, families can establish an inter-vivos (living) trust for a minor, provided the funds are used solely for the benefit of that minor. This trust has one main advantage over a UGMA. The trustee has control over the funds until the "donee" is 21 years old—well into the college paying years

Crummey Trust. Named for the court case under which it originated, this is very similar to the 2503(c) trust described above, but with one important exception. The recipient of the trust (presumably your child) may withdraw any contributions made to the trust in that year. If your child makes no withdrawals, the contribution is added to the principal (and if your child does something stupid with the money, you can stop adding to the trust). The trust may continue as long as the trustee chooses.

Individuals may also each make a tax-free gift of up to $10,000 to either of these two trusts. The drawbacks? You'll need an attorney, and as much as $2,500 in attorney fees to set up a trust and, you'll have to file separate income tax returns for them. Worst of all, recent tax law changes resulted in trust income being taxed far more heavily than individual income. The idea was to nab the rich. Unfortunately, many of the affected trusts are those set up to care for the disabled or to pay for college. Unless there's a change, the first $1,600 in trust income is taxed at 15%; the next $2,200 is taxed at 28%; the next $2,000 is taxed at 31%, the next $2,100 at 36% and anything above $7,900 is taxed at 39.6%.

Charitable Remainder Unitrust. You donate a set amount of money (usually at least $50,000) to a college or a charitable institution, such as your alma mater or local art museum, but stipulate that from 5% to 10% of the value of the gift, be paid out each year as income to a fund for your college-bound student. At the end of a designated time frame, the principal goes to the college or charity. Meanwhile, you, the donor (1) receive a substantial tax deduction (2) build a college fund for junior and (3) give money to a favored charity. Many people choose to donate an appreciated asset for the trust to sell, because that way they avoid paying tax on the appreciation, yet they get to deduct the full market value of the item. You'll need professional help to set up such a trust.

"Spigot" Trust. A variation of the above except you can turn the annual payout on or off. In other words, parents can give up the income during the early years to build up the investment and withdraw extra money in later years when they need money for college. Spigot trusts frequently invest in tax-deferred variable annuities and are packaged with life insurance. For more information, contact your insurance agent.

CDS AND T-BILLS

Some of the safest, and easiest ways for parents to save money are through short- and long-term Certificates of Deposit, Treasury bills (which mature in 13, 26 or 52 weeks), Treasury notes (which mature in 1 to 10 years), Treasury bonds (which mature in 10 to 30 years), and US savings bonds. As you shop around for rates, remember brokerage firms can usually get you the highest rates on CDs and money-market funds. In August, 1996, you could get six-month CDs that yield 5.76%, five-year CDs that yield 6.87%, three-month Treasury bills at 5.29%, one-year bills at 5.83%, two-year Treasury notes at 6.28%, five-year notes at 6.71%, ten-year notes at 6.93%, and 30-year Treasury bonds at 7.1%. Treasuries are exempt from state and local taxes, so for most families, these yields are even higher.

EE SAVINGS BONDS

Parents who have purchased EE savings bonds will not have to pay tax on the interest that accrues, provided the bonds are used to pay for their children's education. Full benefits are available to couples with incomes of $65,250 or less and to single parents with incomes of $43,500 or less when it's time to redeem their bonds. The exemption tapers off for families with incomes above these limits, and disappears completely for couples with incomes above $95,250 and single parents with incomes above $58,500. Income limitations will be indexed for inflation, so, by the time you redeem your bonds, the income ceilings may be much higher. One Catch: Your income for the year in which you plan to redeem your bonds includes all the interest the bonds have earned! This additional income may push some families right past the income cut-offs and ironically eliminate their exclusion! Bonds may be purchased at any time during the year, but the purchasers must be at least 24 years of age. In other words, families with incomes too high to benefit from the tax break may not have their children take advantage of the benefit by buying the bonds themselves. For the same reason, grandparents and couples who file separate tax returns are also ineligible to participate. If you mistakenly bought the bonds in your child's name, you can plead your case by filing a reissue form (PD F 4000) with the Bureau of Public Debt, Savings Bond Operations Office, 200 Third Street, Parkersburg, WV 26106-1328.

EE Bonds no longer carry a guaranteed minimum interest rate. Instead, the interest rate for bonds held less than five years equals 85% of six-month T-bills; the interest rate for bonds held longer than five years equals 85% of five-year Treasury bonds. Rates are adjusted twice a year (May 1 and November 1) and currently stand at 4.36% for the first five years, 4.85% thereafter. For rate information after November 1, call 800-4US BOND.

Note: Interest on EE bonds is posted just twice a year, so time your redemptions carefully otherwise you could lose out on as much as six-month's worth of interest. Bonds are available through payroll deductions and at most banks and credit unions. For more information, get a copy of *The Savings Bond Question and Answer Book* and *Questions and Answers About Education Savings Bonds* from the Department of Treasury, US Savings Bonds Division, Washington, DC 20226.

INFLATION BONDS

For people who worry about the impact of inflation on the value of their bonds, Uncle Sam has introduced a new product, bonds which have yields pegged to the inflation rate. Details are still being finalized, but they will probably be sold as ten-year notes and 30-year bonds, and be available in denominations as low as $1,000. Are they a good idea? Yes, if inflation rises. No, if inflation declines. Your guess is as good as ours.

MUTUAL FUNDS

The best way for small investors to play the market is via a mutual fund. By having your money pooled with money from lots of other investors, you gain the advantage of diversification and professional fund management. Mutual funds are usually categorized by their investment goals. For example, *Growth Funds* aim to increase the value of your investment rather than provide you with a large stream of dividends. Growth Funds generally invest in stocks and are best suited for people who plan to hold on to the fund for a longer period of time, for example, people who won't need to tap their college fund for many years. *Income Funds* focus on providing investors with high current income (i.e., large dividends). Income funds generally invest in corporate and government bonds, or stocks with good dividend-paying records. They bring higher yields than money market funds, but their share price can move up or down, making them a little riskier. *Money Market Funds* are very safe, and accordingly, offer the investor the lowest return. Money Market Funds generally invest in high quality securities with short maturities (e.g., bank CDs, US Treasury bills). Other types of funds include hybrids of the above, for example, Aggressive Growth, Balanced Growth, and Growth and Income. Investors will also find specialty funds grouped by company type (for example, energy, environmental, health care, real estate, utilities, etc.).

For a directory of nearly 5,400 mutual funds (in 21 different investment categories), send $8.50 to the Investment Company Institute, 1401 H Street NW, #1200, Washington DC 20005. The Institute also publishes a series of free brochures on investing with mutual funds, including *Planning for College? The Mutual Fund Advantage Becomes a Parent.*

You can either buy funds yourself (using data from the Institute, the *Wall Street Journal*, or magazines like *Smart Money, Kiplinger's* and *Money)* or, work with a broker. You can even buy "Life-Cycle Funds" which are pre-fabbed allocation pies sold by mutual fund companies; there's a pie for every investment goal.

This tip from the *WSJ*: To simplify your taxes, set up four separate funds. Then, to cover each year's college expenses, sell one fund. Also remember, as students approach college age, families should lower their investment risk by shifting the balance of their savings from aggressive growth funds to growth and income funds, and finally, to money market funds.

ZERO COUPON BONDS

These are municipal bonds, corporate bonds, and treasury bonds stripped of their interest coupons. Owners receive no income while holding the bonds. Instead, the income is compounded semi-annually and reinvested. At some future date, you receive a fixed sum that is considerably larger than your purchase price. For example, a 7.4% zero maturing in 2005, will cost you $486 per thousand, which means you pay $4,860 today to get $10,000 ten years from now. A $10,000 bond maturing in twenty years will cost you only $2,015.

Zero coupons are seldom called "zero coupons." Instead, investors should look for them under acronyms like STRIPS (Separate Trading of Registered Interest and Principal of Securities), TIGRS (Treasury Investment Growth Receipts), CATS (Certificates of Accrual on Treasury Securities), and M-CATS (with "M" standing for Municipal).

Many families like to use zero coupon bonds to save for college expenses because they can time the maturity dates to coincide with their students' tuition bills. Also, they know exactly how much money they will receive when those tuition bills come due, a certainty that for some families is more important than taking chances with a riskier portfolio. There are, however, several drawbacks to zeros, which families should consider before deciding on this type of long-term monetary investment.

- Corporate bonds and municipal bonds may be called before they reach maturity, and if you miss the call, you may be in for a nasty surprise when you go to claim your money. Here's why. When a bond is called (usually because of declining interest rates) interest stops accumulating, and its value freezes. The $10,000 face value you thought you were getting could turn out to be little more than the bond's original cost. Treasury bonds are much safer, as they carry a no-call provision.

- Even though no income is distributed, tax must be paid yearly on the accrued interest. The exception is for zero-coupon municipals which are tax free (but somewhat rare).
- There is no way of knowing what the value of the money will be when the bond matures. If interest rates rise, the value of the bond drops. If interest rates drop, the value of the bond rises. As a rule, corporate bonds have the highest yield, but also the highest risk.
- Will the bond's issuer will be around in 20 years to pay off the amount due? To be safe, avoid bonds issued by small municipalities and corporate bonds with risky ratings (AAA is good, DDD is not). To be extra safe, buy government-backed Treasury zeros.

PREPAID TUITION PLANS

While sophisticated investors can earn greater returns on their own than they can with prepaid tuition plans, the fact is, most families are not comfortable playing investment games. They want an easy way to guarantee they'll have enough money for their children's education, and many families are happy to sacrifice a percentage point or two of interest to buy that security.

State Plans

To encourage early planning for college costs, many states sponsor "Prepaid Tuition Plans" in which parents can guarantee four years of tuition at any of the state's public (or in some cases, private) colleges by making a lump sum investment or periodic payments. (FL allows participants to use the money at any college in the country while MA allows anyone in the country to invest in MA). No two plans are the same, but most operate under the same assumptions: The investment amount depends on the child's date of entry into college, the percentage of costs the family wants to cover, and the degree of flexibility parents desire in withdrawing funds. The state invests the money and pays the student's tuition when he or she enters college, and takes the risk of actually guaranteeing tuition. Families pay tax on the appreciation when they redeem the money for college. As for the interim tax consequences, after a recent court ruling that investment gains inside Michigan's plan could not be taxed, the IRS has dropped the issue. This is good news for all the states that had passed enabling legislation, but were waiting for a definitive tax ruling before starting their program. See Chapter 11 for a state listing and more information.

The College Savings Bank

The College Savings Bank in Princeton offers a similar type of tuition guarantee The Bank sells CDs based on the average cost of 500 independent colleges. The interest rate is 1.5% lower than the average annual tuition increase at these colleges. In other words, if the index rises by 7.61%, the interest rate is 6.11%. Your upfront premium reduces the effective rate of your investment a percentage or so more, making the actual yield not much higher than most passbook savings accounts. Participants in this plan also face steep penalties for early withdrawal; 10% of principal during the first three years, 5% thereafter. For more information on CollegeSure CDs, call 1-800-888-2723, http://www.collegesavings.com.

LIFE INSURANCE

Many people are completely (and justifiably) confused by the endless variety of life insurance options. Essentially there are two types: Term, which provides protection for a fixed period of time but has no cash value (unless you die); and Permanent, which provides lifelong protection, including a death benefit and savings component and does have a cash value if you decide to give up your policy. This second type of insurance is frequently touted as a good vehicle for long term saving needs (like college) and comes in three forms: Whole Life, in which premiums remain constant over the life of the policy; Universal Life in which premiums are flexible subject to certain minimums and maximums; and Variable Life in which death benefits and cash values vary with the performance of your portfolio (and you get to choose from a selection of portfolios). Variable Life gets the most attention from consumer-oriented investment writers since it provides investors with the most flexibility. It is also, however, the riskiest and if you can't invest for at least 15 years, it's unlikely that compounding will ever make the investment worthwhile. In fact, you should be very careful about using any type of cash value life insurance to save for college—only use it when you're certain to maintain the policy for a long time, otherwise fees and commissions will probably make the surrender value worth little more than your initial investment. *In any case, don't decide to invest in life insurance while under pressure or because of tax laws or financial aid rules that place the value of your insurance outside the need analysis formula.*

Another important point. Uniform disclosure is sadly missing in the insurance biz so in evaluating contracts, be certain you compare three things—the costs of the contract (monthly charges, first year charges, and surrender penalties), the performance of the funds in the contract (ask to see the returns after all costs have been deducted) and the cost of the life insurance coverage. Also, be certain you're comparing apples and apples. If one company shows you comparisons making its policy look significantly better than another's, be certain both were calculated using the same market assumptions (e.g., supportable rates of return, mortality rates and expenses). Finally, buy only from highly rated companies (Look for A. M. Best reports in your library for ratings of the insurance industry).

Useful Resources:
- Prospective buyers of life insurance might consider a service offered by the National Insurance Consumer's Organization. For a fee (around $35-$40), NICO will analyze a policy and help you compare it to others. NICO, 703/549-8050.
- Some insurance companies provide advice on college selection and financing. Although they'll probably be happy to sell you insurance (if you need it), the planning service is free, as is the phone call: American National Life Insurance (800/777-2372) and Occidental Life Insurance (800/334-4324) both sponsor Collegiate Planning Centers, and will refer you to lenders for the Stafford Loan.
- The American Council of Life Insurance publishes a good intro to insurance products, *What You Should Know About Buying Life Insurance.* Call 800/942-4242.

CATTLE FUTURES

Just kidding. Hillary may have parlayed $1,000 into $100,000 over ten short months, but the commodities market is a little too volatile and way too mysterious for this brief an overview of investment strategies.

IN WHOSE NAME—PARENT OR CHILD?

As we mentioned earlier, the critical decision you must make in any long-range capital accumulation plan is whether the plan will be in your name, at your tax rate, or in the child's name, at the child's tax rate. The money will grow more quickly in the child's name because of the lower tax bracket. But when it comes time to pay tuition bills, the child's money is subject to a much heavier assessment. Colleges will demand 35% of the child's assets each year, but only 5.6% of parental assets.

Let's attach some numbers. A family in the 35% bracket (this includes an allowance for state taxes) elects to make a yearly gift of $1,000 to a child, starting at birth. The money is invested at 8%. At the end of eighteen years, the kitty will be worth $34,892. Had the family added $1,000 per year to a parental account, also invested at 8%, the money, under higher taxation, would have grown to only $28,662.

Now it's need analysis/family contribution time. For each of the next four years, the student's kitty is depleted by 35% of its value. The parental kitty, on the other hand, is depleted by only 5.6%. At the end of four years, the child's kitty has shrunk by $28,664 to $6,228. The parental kitty has shrunk by only $5,904 and is still a respectable $22,758.

So what should you do?

If there is no chance your family will qualify for aid, save in the child's name, the money will accumulate more quickly. To take advantage of the fact that unearned income of children over 14 is still taxed at the child's rate, if you have young children, your gifts should take the form of tax-deferred investments, such as US Savings Bonds and fast growing stocks. Once the child reaches 14, redeem the bonds, sell the stocks, and place the proceeds in a safe, but high yielding investment. Then spend it all on tuition.

If there is any chance for getting aid, save in the parent's name, make the smaller family contribution, and pad your college expenditures with need based aid.

Predicting aid eligibility is no easy task. Constantly changing tax laws and student assistance laws confuse professionals, to say nothing of those whose jobs do not depend on keeping up with Congressional activity. Here's what we advise. Assume the ratio between present earnings and assets and present college costs will hold for the future. Run your family through the Federal Methodology in Appendix 1. Compare the estimated family contribution with the current costs of colleges of interest. If your family contribution is less than the cost of college today, you may qualify for aid in the future. Remember to divide the parental contribution by the number you will have in college at least half-time at any one time.

CONFUSED? STRANGLED BY LOOPHOLES AND RED TAPE?

If you're running into snags or all these techniques are confusing or require too much research, then request our free brochure *We Can Help* (Octameron, PO Box 2748, Alexandria, VA 22301). It describes our college admission and financial aid services. Neither cost very much and both can save you a bundle—both in money and in time.

Our Tuesday Special. We keep an experienced counselor on the phone nearly every Tuesday from 10 a.m. until 4 p.m. EST, to answer questions you may have about college financing (or selection or admission). The conversation will cost you $30 which you may charge against your VISA or MasterCard. Call (703) 836-5480.

Part IV
The Major Money Sources

Chapter 9
The Colleges

RETHINKING YOUR IDEAS ABOUT ADMISSION

Unless you plan to attend one of the few highly selective colleges, banish the thought that it's hard to get into college. It's easy. Over 92% of all students are accepted by their first or second choice school. In the old days, you applied to five or six schools; one or two where your odds were fifty-fifty, a couple where you had the edge, and a safety school that was sure to take you. Today your selection strategy needs to be based on factors other than the possibility of rejection. First and foremost you should consider quality of education and your fit with each school, but then you should consider its financial aid offerings. Look for:

1. Schools with innovative payment plans. These can ease cash flow problems.
2. Schools with innovative aid programs. These can funnel money toward "desirable" students.
3. Schools with mountains of cash. These can usually handle your "need."
4. Schools with a reputation for leadership in your selected field of study. They are likely to be well-endowed in your field.

FINANCIAL AID IN THE ADMISSION PROCESS

If students can't afford the school, they aren't going to enroll! This simple truth means that at many schools, the line between financial aid and admission is beginning to disappear. New experiments in "enrollment management" and the intense competition for quality students translate into "no-need" awards and "preferential packaging." In other words, aid administrators are being pressured to reassess family contributions and the contents of aid packages for certain students to help the school meet enrollment goals. At most schools, however, aid resources are limited so the first people in line are still more likely to have their need met than the last. Given these words of wisdom, it's up to you to take action.

1. Apply "early decision" for both admission and financial aid—that way you should have all your need met.
2. Apply to colleges where your qualifications place you in the upper 25% of the applicant pool. That standing will have a significant impact on the composition of your aid package. Schools make no bones about that. Oberlin (OH), for example, says its "policy is to award financial aid packages with larger portions of grant aid to those students who show great academic promise or who can contribute to the College's diversity. This policy is consistent with Oberlin's goal of maintaining a high-quality academic program and attracting a talented and diverse student body."
3. Always pair your applications. For better "leverage," apply to two four-star schools; and two three-star schools; not just one of each. This may increase your application fees, however, when you receive acceptances from schools of similar prestige, you may be able to use that to improve your aid package. A school may not mind losing you to a lesser or higher regarded college. But it will fight to keep you from going to a competitor

IT DOESN'T HURT TO ASK

The financial aid sections of college catalogues are often very vague. Pious generalities outnumber hard facts while the tone is reminiscent of sweepstakes notices. Why do schools do this? First of all, vagueness about financial aid is important when you know Uncle Sam will release some enormous rule change two days after 500,000 copies of your school's materials come back from the printer. Second, it's hard to be precise about what kinds of aid a student might expect when financial aid decisions vary from student to student depending on the their income and asset situation and their admission qualifications. And third, the "you may be a grand prize winner" attitude is essential for colleges trying to convince students not to worry about the $25,000 bill they'll face if they enroll! While it's true that aid packages at many schools are quite generous (Princeton, for example, awards $19 million per year from its own scholarship funds), frequently, that generosity takes the form of loans, which you must repay.

There are exceptions. Saint Olaf (MN) says, "We believe the primary responsibility for meeting college costs at Saint Olaf rests with the student and the family. Because going to college is an experience that is out of the ordinary, it sometimes also requires some out of the ordinary financial sacrifices." Princeton (NJ) explains, "(We) assign low-interest loans as part of a financial aid award because (we) believe a student should be willing to invest in his or her future." And Central College (IA) made no bones about using aid for recruiting. "Frankly, we're out to attract talented and academically-ambitious students and we'll reward them for their past performance as well as for their potential."

But such candor is seldom found. To get answers, you will have to write. Don't be bashful. You have the right to ask colleges as many questions as they ask you. Find out about innovative payment plans of the type illustrated in the next two sections. And get answers to the following questions:

1. Do you guarantee to meet a student's financial need (or a certain percentage of a student's need)? *Reason*: Under the Federal Methodology, many more families are eligible for financial aid. Unfortunately, additional federal money has not been appropriated to help all these newly eligible families.

2. Do you have a per-student-limit on the aid you provide? *Reason*: Some schools set ceilings, such as a $10,000 per student maximum.

3. Do I have to demonstrate a minimum amount of need to qualify for aid? *Reason*: Some schools won't consider students for aid unless they have at least $500 need.

4. Do you have a standard "unmet need" figure for each aid recipient? Reason: Some schools will, automatically, leave each aid recipient $500 short.

5. What is your expected "student earnings" figure? *Reason*: Regardless of the results of need analysis, some colleges expect a certain amount (which can be as high as $1,700 per year). The colleges will expect that amount, whether it comes from the student's contribution or the parents' contribution.

6. Is there an application cut-off date for guaranteeing a student's unmet need? *Reason*: Some colleges say they can meet all need for students whose applications are received prior to Date X. But no such guarantee extends to students who apply after that.

7. Do you maintain financial aid "waiting lists" or accept students on an "admit-deny" basis? *Reason*: These practices mean financially needy students are welcome but they will not receive financial aid.

8. If I don't apply for aid in my freshman year, can I apply in subsequent years? *Reason*: You can't be prohibited from applying, however, you may get nothing because many colleges give priority to "continuing recipients."
9. How are "outside scholarships" packaged? *Reason*: Different colleges have different "aid philosophies." One school in New York will take the first $300 of the outside scholarship and 20% of the rest and use it to replace a loan. What's left reduces the student's grant from that school. At other colleges, the outside scholarship merely replaces, on a dollar for dollar basis, collegiate grants, causing the poet Leider to ponder from her garret:

You found a nifty scholarship
To loosen the tuition grip.
But does this change what you must pay?
Or do they take your grant away?

Don't expect outside scholarships to lower family contribution. According to federal regulations, no-need scholarships cannot be used in that manner (unless, as explained in Chapter 7, the scholarship exceeds the amount of your financial need). But do search for a policy that at least permits it to replace part of the package's self-help component (loans and work-study).
10. What percentage of alumni contribute to the school's annual fundraising campaign? *Reason*: If you are worried about the college's financial survival, you can't ask for a corporate balance sheet. But you can check with the college's development office to learn whether the school has strong alumni support. At some schools, it's as high as 65% and when colleges have this kind of loyalty, they are not going to fold.

SIXTEEN INNOVATIVE PAYMENT PLANS

1. **Installment Plans.** Realizing not many people can write a $5,000 or $10,000 check at the beginning of each semester, many colleges soften the blow by letting you spread the payments. Furthermore, by taking advantage of installment plans, you may not have to borrow as much as you originally thought. If a college doesn't have a plan of its own, ask whether it works with Academic Management Service (800-635-0120), Knight Payment Plan (800-225-6783), or Tuition Management Systems (800-722-4867). AMS alone has contracts with 1,500 schools, but sometimes you have to ask the right person the right question to find out. Here are variants you may encounter.
   - Interest: (1) No interest (2) Fixed interest (3) Interest on the remaining balance (4) No interest, but a one-time fee.
   - Down Payment: (1) No down payment (2) Down payment of 1/3 or 1/4.
   - Payment Frequency: (1) Ten monthly installments (2) Two installments per semester (3) Four installments per semester.
2. **Prepayment Discount.** Pay a year all at once, and your tuition is discounted, sometimes by as much as 10%.
3. **Advance Payment Bonus.** Place money into your account before it's due and the college adds a bonus to your balance. It can be a set dollar amount (e.g., $100) or it can be a percentage of the amount on deposit (e.g., 2%).
4. **Adjustable Rate Loans.** First we had adjustable rate mortgages; now colleges are offering adjustable rate tuition loans. Sometimes the amount of your monthly payment changes with the rate. Other times, the size of your monthly payment remains the same, but because neither the total amount borrowed nor interest rates can be predicted—both tuition costs and interest rates

fluctuate—borrowers will not know how long they must make their payments. All they know is that the payments will continue long after graduation.

5. **Tuition Freezes.** A guarantee that tuition will hold for a set time or that it won't increase by more than a fixed percentage (e.g., 3%). Some schools use freezes to improve retention and limit them to 3rd and 4th year students.

6. **Guaranteed Tuition Plans I.** No Prepayment. Guarantees students their tuition will not be increased in their sophomore, junior, and senior years.

7. **Guaranteed Tuition Plans II.** Deposit Required. Same as preceding plan, but the college requires you to maintain a set sum on deposit—anywhere from $500 to $3,000. These plans may a have a financing option.

8. **Guaranteed Tuition Plans III.** Prepayment Required. Pay four years tuition in advance, at the rate which prevails your freshman year. Parents who can make an out-of-pocket prepayment must decide whether the tuition increases they will be spared are worth more than what their money could earn in interest if it had not been used for prepayment. If the money is to be borrowed, parents usually have two choices: (1) The sponsoring college will act as lender, offering money at a favorable interest rate. Repayment may extend from four to fifteen years. (2) Parents might raise the money by borrowing against the equity in their house. The interest rate may or may not be higher than the rate offered by the college. One advantage is that interest payments on home equity loans of up to $100,000 are tax deductible.

9. **Guaranteed Tuition Plans IV.** Other Types. At some schools, the guaranteed tuition plan covers as many years as parents can pay in advance—one, two, three, or four. At others, the school will sweeten the pot by rebating say 10% of the payment at the end of each year.

10. **Stretched Payments.** Not unlike a loan. Parents of students who do not qualify for aid defer a fixed amount of their tuition bill. They are given two years to pay the deferred amount and are charged a slight interest rate.

11. **Barter.** A usable service provided by you or your parents is exchanged for tuition.

12. **Three-Year Option.** Some colleges offer a "time-shortened degree option" that permits students to meet graduation requirements in three years, saving one year in tuition costs.

13. **Two Degrees in One.** Students can also save a year's tuition by finding schools that offer joint undergraduate-graduate degree programs. For example, students can receive their BA-MBA in five years instead of the usual six, or a BA-MA in four years instead of the usual five.

14. **Choice of Accommodations and Meal Plans.** Do you need a spacious room with a spectacular view, or are you happy contemplating the backside of a dumpster? Do you need 21 meals a week in the dining hall or would you rather fend for yourself when the menu reads "Chef's Surprise" or "Mystery Meat?" Colleges give you options. Some colleges have housing contracts that vary up to $2,000 per year, depending on location and type of room. Others offer several different meal plans. Cost difference: from $25 to $1,000 per year.

15. **Use of Credit Cards for Bill Payment.** Provides credit card holders with some flexibility but can cost them dearly in finance charges. If you pay by this option, you might consider using an "affinity" credit card that at least gives you a bonus, like frequent flier miles. Or, use the college's own card.

16. **Use of Electronic Bank Transfers.** A set amount is transferred directly from your account to the college each month.

THIRTY SIX INNOVATIVE AID PROGRAMS

1. **Academic Scholarships.** Over 1200 colleges and universities offer scholarships—generally of the "no-need" type—to students who meet special criteria in grade point averages, SAT/ACT scores, or class standing. See *The A's & B's of Academic Scholarships* (inside back cover).

2. **Research Assistants.** Some (hoity-toity) colleges claim not to offer merit-based awards, because if they did, "all of their students would deserve one." Some of these schools do, however, offer the students they most want to enroll special financial incentives, like research jobs with their choice of faculty (complete with large stipends) or high-paying summer internships.

3. **Low Interest Loans.** Many colleges have become low-interest lenders to offset Uncle Sam's yo-yo student aid policies and provide parents with financial planning stability.

4. **Quickie Loans.** Many colleges offer short term loans to tide students over in times of temporary financial crisis. These loans usually run from $100 to $500, but sometimes students can get up to $5,000.

5. **Replacing Loans.** Many schools let you use outside scholarships to replace the loan component of your aid package. Some schools limit this bonus to bright students, or convert your loan to a grant only if you maintain a certain GPA. Others make the switch only if you find the scholarship before your loan gets processed. You should also ask if the school has a limit (e.g., $2,000) on the total amount it will replace.

6. **Middle Income Assistance Programs.** Special loans and scholarships for middle-income families.

7. **Asset-Rich Families.** Land-rich families whose holdings are "non-liquid" but disqualify them for assistance can sometimes get special consideration.

8. **Family Plans.** Rebates or lower tuitions when more than one family member enrolls. And that includes not only brother and sister, but also Mom, Dad and Grandma. Examples: Trinity College (DC) gives a 33% discount to additional family members. Santa Clara (CA) gives free tuition to the first of three enrolled at the same time.

9. **Alumni Children.** Tuition breaks for alumni kids are also common. Colleges like to establish multi-generation relationships with families. That's how chairs get endowed and buildings get built.

10. **Peace of Mind.** Some schools waive (or reduce) tuition if the person primarily responsible for the student's support dies or suffers total disability.

11. **Incentives for Academic Achievement.** Many colleges have special awards for the top enrolled (continuing) students. Other schools offer academic awards to any student who was in the top 10% of their high school class. Finally, some schools will convert part of a student's loans to grants if the student maintains a high GPA.

12. **Matching Scholarships.** Some schools match church scholarships. Other schools match state regents awards, or Dollars for Scholars awards.

13. **Remissions for Student Leaders.** Many colleges provide discounts to campus leaders, for example, student government officers, school newspaper editors. You won't get this money your first year, but you should know about it so that you can start planning your campaign for student body president.

14. **Remissions for Work.** At Warren Wilson (NC) and Blackburn (IL) students get free room and board. But they must put in fifteen hours of campus work every week. Berea (KY) charges no tuition to students of limited means, but

requires them to work ten hours/week. Many other schools provide room and board for residence hall assistants and supervisors. You may not qualify in your first year, but it's an opportunity you should know about.

15. **Emphasis on Student Employment.** Many colleges have beefed up their placement offices to help students find on- and off-campus employment. Bluffton College (OH) budgeted over $300,000 for campus employment in a "Learn & Earn" program. Princeton (NJ) assisted students who want to become entrepreneurs. Cornell (NY), in a massive program, offered over 400 students $2,000 work grants in the hope of reducing their dependence on loans. Schools like Amherst (MA) use their formidable alumni network to locate student summer work opportunities. St. Edward's University (TX) entered into an agreement with a major retail chain for hundreds of part-time jobs. A special benefit of this program: It conserves federal work-study funds.

16. **Off-Hour Rates.** Many colleges set lower credit hour charges for courses taken during off-hours—evenings, weekends and summers. The difference can be as high as $300 per course or a 50% reduction in room rates (for summer school).

17. **Moral Obligation Scholarships.** Not a scholarship. Not a loan. The college provides money to the student and attaches a moral—but not legal—obligation to pay it back after graduation. A special sweetener: Until IRS changes its rules, the pay-back becomes a gift to the college and a tax deduction to the former student.

18. **Trial Attendance.** Some colleges say, "Try us you'll like us" and will offer new students a discount on their first few credits. For example, the school may offer free classes to high school juniors and seniors, it may let some students try the school for one semester for a low fee (e.g., $25), or it may run a free summer program to give students a little taste.

19. **Bucking the Trend.** Some colleges seek to win the enrollment competition by freezing or even lowering tuition.

20. **Special Scholarship Drives.** Some schools have launched special fundraising drives aimed at increasing their in-house financial aid kitty. Columbia University (NY) raises $100,000 a year from Visa and Master card users through a collaboration with MBNA America Bank.

21. **Helping Students Find Scholarships.** Hundreds of schools have special offices to help students find grants, scholarships, etc.

22. **Older Student Remissions.** If you are over 24, some schools will give you a discount on tuition, however, at most school, "older" means 50 or 60. In fact, many public schools offer free tuition to senior citizens as long as they are state residents and attend on a space available basis.

23. **Special Students.** Colleges look for students with unique interests or backgrounds. Many give special scholarships to any member of the National Honor Society or students who want to be math or science teachers. Grand Canyon (AZ) is looking for Eagle Scouts. Tarleton State (TX) offers rodeo scholarships. And, Arkansas College (AR) will pay you to play the bagpipes.

24. **Persistence Awards.** Schools used to worry about retention rates. Now they worry about student persistence. The name may have changed (a feeble effort by educators to shift responsibility for retention from school to student) but the concept hasn't. To recoup all the money they spend recruiting new students, schools must keep them enrolled (and paying at least some tuition) for four years. Accordingly, to keep you from transferring or dropping out,

some colleges offer financial inducements such as cancelling part of your loans or considering you for extra scholarships.

25. **Travel Awards.** Some schools want to repay you either for a campus visit or, if you are enrolled, for your commuting costs.

26. **Loan Origination Fee.** Stafford Loans carry a 3% origination fee. Some schools will pay your origination fee.

27. **Adopt-a-Student.** At some schools, local churches and community groups help students with scholarship money. Other schools work with local businesses (some companies even extend interest-free loans to students that are forgiven if the student, after graduation, goes to work for the sponsor).

28. **Students Helping Students.** When that happens, it's a sign of good student morale and a friendly campus. Some examples we've heard about recently: At DePauw (IN), students raised $134,00 for scholarships in a phonathon. At Brown (RI), the University put $4 in the college's scholarship fund for every hour student volunteers spent picking up litter on campus. At Georgetown (DC) students have organized a credit union and at Guilford (NC) students have raised over $100,000 to start a loan fund of their own. At Notre Dame (IN) students waived return of room-damage deposits, electing to contribute the money to a scholarship fund. Fitchburg State (MA) deposited all parking fines in a scholarship fund. And Davidson's (NC) senior class gift to the college was a $100,000 scholarship fund.

29. **Running Start.** High school students can spend their senior year, or the summer before their senior year on a campus, taking regular college classes. Colleges look on such students as a farm club. For example, at Wesley (DE), any local student in the top 40% of the HS class may take (and receive academic credit for) up to two courses each semester for free. Simon's Rock College (MA) awards 2-year scholarships to HS sophomores. After completing the two year "Acceleration to Excellence" program, students have the option of completing their BA at Simon's Rock for the cost of attending their home-state public university. No matter what program is offered, here are some questions to ask: Are the courses for college credit? If so, are the credits good only at the offering college or are they transferable?

30. **Help for the Unemployed.** Some schools offer free tuition to students from families whose major wage earner is unemployed.

31. **Free Tuition for Farmers.** Some schools offer up to a year of free tuition to farmers who have had to quit farming because of financial hardships.

32. **A Birthday Gift.** To celebrate its 100th anniversary, Dana (NE) let each graduating senior award a $4,000 scholarship to any incoming student. Goucher (MD) celebrated its 100th birthday by allowing selected students to pay 1885 tuition rates, $100/year. Note: Both of these opportunities are past, but keep your eyes open for similar "celebrations."

33. **Guaranteed Degree.** Some schools allow graduates who are unhappy with their major (because they couldn't find a job, maybe) to return to the alma mater and major in another field, tuition-free, or at least at reduced tuition. One school, Saint Norbert College promises that if a student doesn't graduate in four years because the college failed to offer a required class, the school will pay the additional tuition.

34. **Tuition Equalization.** To compete more effectively with public schools for top students, some private colleges offer their own tuition equalization programs. At Bard College (NY), first year students who were in the top ten

of their high school class pay only as much tuition as they would have paid had they gone to their state-supported school. The University of Rochester is giving alumni children and all students from NY State a $5,000 discount on tuition. They hope this will lure students who don't need additional assistance, thus actually save on financial aid expenses.

35. **Toll-Free Numbers.** Hundreds of schools send aid recipients a toll-free number and the name of a "personal financial counselor" with whom to discuss financing options.

36. **Reward for Community Service.** Many schools encourage students to participate in community service. Some even give course credit. Campus Compact, c/o Brown University, Box 1975, Providence, RI 02912 is a coalition of 520 colleges serving 140,000 students. Campus Outreach Opportunity League is a coalition that serves students at nearly 650 schools. (COOL, 1511 K Street NW, #307, Washington, DC 20005, http:// www.cool2serve.org/homeofc/home.html/)

For a more complete listing, get *College CheckMate* (see inside back cover).

IMPACT OF TAX REFORM

Now that we've looked at the variety of innovative payment plans you must understand how their benefits are lessened by three provisions in the tax code:

1. **Interest on Consumer Debt is Not Deductible.** You get no deduction for interest paid on consumer debt (credit cards, auto loans, personal loans). This greatly diminishes the popularity of guaranteed tuition plans as the interest payments on the money most families must borrow to pay four years of tuition in advance is not deductible (unless the family borrows against its home. Interest on mortgage payments is still deductible).

2. **Some Scholarships Taxed As Income.** The portion of a scholarship that exceeds tuition, fees, books and equipment is taxed as ordinary income. This means room and board scholarships may be taxed. If you've received a large grant, use it to pay the tax-free items first, and keep track of everything left over. You're usually on your own to report your good fortune to the IRS.

3. **Graduate Teaching Assistantships Taxed As Income.** Tuition discounts (or tuition payments) received in exchange for services is considered taxable income. The University of Wisconsin (as reported by Jane Bryant Quinn) sums up graduate aid quite nicely: Stipends for teaching assistantships are taxable because the work helps the school without being central to a student's studies. Stipends for research assistants are tax free because the research, while of interest to the student and the teacher, isn't necessary to the school. Fellowships are clean—no work, no tax.

THE RICH SCHOOLS

Rich schools generally have more funds for student aid than poor schools. At some, the average need-based grant ranges from $10,000 to $15,000! Rich schools also have greater flexibility in making financial aid awards. It's their money, so they are better able to take individual circumstances into account than schools that dispense, in the main, public funds. Wealth can be judged in one of two ways: (1) Total endowment or (2) endowment per enrolled student. Here are schools with mountains of money:

Over $2 billion: Harvard, U. of Texas System, Yale, Princeton, Stanford, Emory, Texas A&M System, Columbia, U. of California, MIT, Washington U..

Over $1 billion: U. of Pennsylvania, Rice, Cornell, Northwestern, U. of Chicago, U. of Michigan .

Over $400 million: Notre Dame, Dartmouth, U. of Southern California, Johns Hopkins, U. of Virginia, Duke, New York U., U. of Minnesota, CalTech, U. of Rochester, Brown, Case Western, Rockefeller U., Purdue, Ohio State, Swarthmore, Wellesley, U. of Delaware, Smith, Boston College, Macalester, U. of Cincinnati, Southern Methodist, Grinnell, U. of Pittsburgh, Carnegie-Mellon, Indiana U., U. of Richmond, Texas Christian, Pomona, Williams, Wake Forest, and Georgetown

Endowment per student leads to different rankings. Rockefeller U., Princeton, Harvard, CalTech, Rice, Grinnell, Swarthmore, Yale.

LEADERSHIP IN SELECTED FIELDS

Colleges that are acknowledged leaders in selected disciplines (e.g., the Midwestern colleges in agriculture; the western schools in mining and geology) are usually heavily endowed by private sponsors in the areas of their special expertise. You are far more likely to find an agriculture scholarship at Iowa State than at Baruch College in New York City, or a petroleum engineering scholarship at the University of Oklahoma than at the University of the District of Columbia.

For opinions on who is best in what, ask the guidance office or school library to pick up a copy of **Rugg's Recommendations on the Colleges** ($19.95, Rugg's Recommendations, 7120 Serena Court, Atascadero, CA 93422). Another (perhaps better) way to get this kind of information is to speak with people you respect in your intended academic/career field. Find out where they went to school, and ask if they have any recommendations.

A tip: Strong departments usually have funds they control themselves rather than the financial aid office. Consider dropping a note to the department head and ask about the possibility of departmental assistance.

WORKING WITH FINANCIAL AID ADMINISTRATORS

The median salary of financial aid directors in 1995/96 was $45,400. You might keep that sum in mind as you get ready to explain how your $100,000 income has been ravaged by inflation to the point of making it impossible—absolutely impossible—to handle your family contribution. Interestingly (but not surprisingly), studies show that with low-income families, willingness to pay exceeds their ability, while with high income families, ability to pay exceeds their willingness.

Remember that financial aid administrators primarily dispense public funds—tax money—and such expenditures are usually strictly controlled by law and regulations. Financial aid administrators do have some flexibility in awarding the colleges' own funds and in treating changed circumstances—such unfortunate events as death, disability, disaster, and divorce. If you feel that any element of your award letter—the student's expense budget, your family contribution, or the mix of aid programs offered—should be changed, then go ahead and call the office. But do so with sound reasons and, if necessary, with documentation. Let them know about better aid offers you have received, but don't take the approach that you're cutting a deal. Financial aid administrators are professionals working with limited funds. If they agree to increase your award, it's frequently at the expense of another's. The FAA will not make that decision lightly, and never without good cause. So before you bully your way into the financial aid office demanding a recount, document your case carefully and keep in mind that one catches more Drosophila Melanogaster with honey than with vinegar.

Chapter 10
Uncle Sam

Every Student's Song
Do not forsake me, oh my Uncle, before commencement day.
Do not change programs, oh my Uncle, oh please, oh please—I say.
I do not know what costs await me, I only know there will be more.
I need to have the grants you give me, or be a drop-out, a lazy drop-out,
Or a starving sophomore.

MEET YOUR UNCLE—UNCLE SAM

For many students, applying for financial aid represents their first encounter with Uncle Sam. One thing will become apparent very quickly. Getting things from Uncle Sam is no more pleasant an experience than giving him things, like your money at tax time. Here is what you should expect:

Uncle Sam likes forms. Lots of forms. Most of the forms have an awkward layout, an illogical sequence, and poorly written instructions.

Uncle Sam makes a sharp distinction between "authorizations" and "appropriations." A program may be authorized, but that doesn't mean a nickel will be spent (appropriated) for it. Be careful when you hear about a much-heralded $10 billion student aid program. Before your expectations get too high, make sure the money for the program has actually been appropriated.

Uncle loves semantics and fine distinctions. His authorization bill may promise a chicken in every pot. But the enabling legislation, usually expressed in regulations, may define "chicken" as "any part of the bird," a claw, a feather... Or the definition may emphasize the avian nature of a chicken. The operative word then becomes "bird" and any bird can be substituted for a chicken—pigeon, crow...

Uncle is a social engineer. After redefining chicken, he will turn his attention to the pot. He may rule that anybody who owns a pot large enough to hold a chicken is too rich to qualify for a fowl. Only owners of small pots can get birds—the smaller the pot, the bigger the bird will seem.

Uncle's promises don't hold for very long. Any program can be supplemented, altered, filibustered, modified or rescinded in mid-year or near election time when it becomes important to hold down expenses and balance the budget.

Uncle likes to arm wrestle with himself. If the Administration doesn't like what Congress has mandated (or vice versa), it will miss deadlines, base its case on budget figures that have already been rejected (but not yet replaced), blow smoke over the issues, hold up regulations, or tie up appropriated funds.

Uncle's timing does not correspond to the academic cycle. When you want to start planning for the next year, usually in September, Uncle is not ready for you. By the time he can tell you what he will do for you, you've already made your plans.

But when all is said and done, Uncle Sam is still your main source of financial aid. Warts or no warts, you had better learn to live with him and like him.

Program	Level of Study		Need-Based		Part-Timers		Need Analysis
	Under-grad	Grad	Yes	No	Yes	No	
Pell Grant	X		X		X		FM
Stafford Loan	X	X	X			X	FM
PLUS Loans	X			X		X	none
Direct Stafford Loan	X	X	X			X	FM
Direct Plus Loan	X			X		X	none
Unsubsidized Stafford	X	X		X		X	FM
SEOG	X		X		X		FM
Work-study	X	X	X		X		FM
Perkins Loans	X	X	X		X		FM

THE BIG SIX TODAY

Most of Uncle's student aid flows through six gigantic programs. Three are student based—Pell Grants, Family Education Loans (Stafford and PLUS), and Direct Student Loans (Direct Stafford and Direct PLUS). You apply for assistance under these programs and the money comes to you.

The other three programs—Supplemental Educational Opportunity Grants, Work-Study and Perkins Loans—are campus-based. This means Uncle funds the programs, but gives the money to the colleges to dispense in accordance with federal guidelines. Most of the money goes to full- and half-time students, however, if the financial need of part-timers is at least 5% of the need of all the students at the school, then at least 5% of campus-based funds must be offered to these students.

Last year, Uncle funded two state-based programs—Byrd Honors Scholarships and State Student Incentive Grants—and one community-based program—AmeriCorps. Unfortunately, these programs may fall to the FY97 budget ax.

Useful Contacts

For information about federal programs, call the Federal Student Aid Information Center, 800-4-FED-AID, Monday through Friday between 9:00 a.m. and 8:00 p.m, EST (TDD: 800-730-8913). Trained staff can help families complete the FAFSA, explain Expected Family Contribution and answer questions about student eligibility. You may also request Uncle's free booklet, *The Student Guide: Financial Aid from the Department of Education.* The number is NOT to be used for financial counseling, to change information in your file, to interpret policy, or to expedite application processing.

To check on the status of your application, or to request a duplicate Student Aid Report, call 319-337-5665. If you suspect fraud or abuse involving federal student aid funds, please call the Inspector General's Office at 800-MIS-USED.

For information about the GI Bill and benefits for dependents of deceased or disabled veterans, call the Department of Veteran's's Affairs, 800-827-1000.

Project EASI (Easy Access for Students and Institutions)

Project EASI is supposed to combine all grant and loan information onto one computer network, accessible to students, parents and colleges. Students will be able to apply for financial aid electronically as well as view their loan history and learn about other aspects of admission and financial aid. It's been slow going, thanks to recent personnel shake-ups in the Department. But the site is partially up and running at http://EASI.ed.gov. You might get better (and more) information at the Department of Education's main site at http://www.ed.gov.

PELL GRANTS

These make up Uncle's largest gift program. In 1996/97, over $5.6 billion in Pells will be dispensed to 3.7 million students. They are the foundation of student aid, the bottom layer of the financial aid package. But they can also be called Pinochio Grants. Why? Because Uncle seldom holds to the award range that he promises. Last year, $2,440 increased to $2,470; before that, $2,400 became $2,340. How does this happen? Easy. Pells are a big part of the Education budget and increasing or decreasing 3.7 million Pells by $50, $100 or $200 can make a big difference in the budget numbers. Last year's last minute increase was a first, perhaps to salve the consciences of over-zealous budget cutters who decimated so many other social safety-net programs. So what will the award range be for 1997/98? Congressional leaders have proposed increasing the top award from $2,470 to $2,500. Our prediction: Pay no attention to authorization bills that say Pells can go up to $4,100 or Administration requests for $2,700. Why are we so pessimistic? Until we come close to balancing our budget, Pell will not be fully funded. Remember, there's a difference between "authorization" and "appropriation."

How large a Pell will you get? It varies with your expected family contribution, the cost of education at your school and your student status. If you are a part-time, half-time or three-quarter time student, you receive 25%, 50% or 75% of your award, respectively. Uncle publishes tables with exact levels of Pell funding, but to get an estimate, if the cost of college exceeds the maximum Pell (e.g., $2,500), just subtract your EFC from the maximum grant. For example, assuming an award range of $400 to $2,500, an EFC of $1,000 translates into $1,500 for full-time students ($750 for half-time students); an EFC of $2,300 gets you nothing.

For Whom the Pell Tolls

You apply for a Pell by completing the FAFSA. Make certain to go this route, even if you're certain you aren't eligible. Colleges and the states expect you to do so and won't consider you for other awards until they know your Pell status. The only way for them to know your Pell status is by seeing results from your FAFSA.

FAMILY EDUCATION LOANS AND DIRECT STUDENT LOANS

Uncle Sam now runs two parallel student loan programs:

Federal Family Education Loans: Subsidized Staffords, Unsubsidized Staffords and PLUS. These loans are made by commercial lenders.

Federal Direct Student Loans: Direct Subsidized Staffords, Direct Unsubsidized Staffords, and Direct PLUS. These loans are made by Uncle Sam.

Interest rates, annual and aggregate loan limits, fees, deferments, cancellations, and forbearance terms are essentially the same. Repayment options vary slightly. The main difference, as far as the student is concerned, is who lends them the money. So why are there two different programs? Politics, as usual. Can you borrow under both? No! Your college will tell you which program it prefers.

Stafford Loans

Formerly called Guaranteed Student Loans, the program was renamed in honor of retired Senator Robert T. Stafford (R-VT). Stafford Loans are low-interest loans to undergraduate and graduate students enrolled at least half-time. They are available to all families without regard to financial need.

Which Stafford Loan is for you?

Students with financial need may receive a subsidized Stafford in which Uncle pays the interest while they are in school and during any deferments.

Students without financial need may receive an unsubsidized Stafford in which interest accrues while they are in school and during any deferments.

Students with partial financial need may receive a combination of the two, depending on their status (dependent vs. independent) and level of need.

Loan Limits:

Dependent Undergraduates: Freshmen may borrow up to $2625 per year. Sophomores may borrow $3500 per year. Juniors, seniors and fifth year undergrads may borrow $5500 per year. The maximum undergraduate loan amount is $23,000. These limits apply whether the money comes from the subsidized or unsubsidized program (or a combination of the two). For example, a freshman who receives a $1500 subsidized Stafford may also borrow $1125 under the unsubsidized program.

Independent Undergraduates: Freshmen may borrow $6625 per year. Sophomores may borrow $7500 per year (in both cases at least $4000 must come from the unsubsidized program). Juniors, seniors and fifth year undergraduates may borrow up to $10,500 per year (of which at least $5000 must come from the unsubsidized program). The maximum an independent student may borrow during his or her undergraduate years is $46,000.

Graduate Students may borrow up to $18,500 per year (of which at least $10,000 must come from the unsubsidized program) to a maximum of $138,500 ($65,500 in subsidized loans, $73,000 in unsubsidized loans). This limit includes any money they borrowed as an undergraduate.

Additional Limits: In no case may a Stafford Loan exceed the cost of attendance at your school minus any other financial aid you receive.

Prorated loan limits: Borrowing limits are prorated for programs of less than a full academic year. For example, students attending the equivalent of 1/3 of an academic year are eligible for 1/3 the maximum annual loan amount.

Loan Origination Fee and Insurance Fees. Commercial lenders subtract a 3% loan origination fee and a 1% insurance fee. As an extra incentive to borrow from them, lenders may soon be allowed to pay your origination fee (on both subsidized and unsubsidized loans) saving you as much as $1,000. If your loan comes from Uncle, you pay a combined 4% instead. No deals.

Interest Rate. The rate is adjusted annually to equal 3.1% more than the bond equivalent of the 91-day T-bill with an 8.25% cap. This year, it is 8.25%.

Interest Subsidy. For families with demonstrated financial need, Uncle Sam pays interest on the loan while the student is in school and for a six-month grace period after the student completes his or her studies.

Minimum Annual Repayment. $600.

Years to Repay. 5 to 10.

Who Makes Loans? Private lenders—Banks, Credit Unions, Insurance Companies. Also Uncle Sam (for students Direct Lending schools).

Application Procedure. Obtain a Common Loan Application and Promissory Note from the lender. Fill out the application. Send it to your school's financial aid administrator for certification. The application then goes back to the lender and guaranteeing agency who will disburse the loan to the school. If your school participates in Direct Lending, you do not need to file an additional application. The aid administrator can certify your eligibility for a Stafford based on results from your FAFSA and ask Uncle to wire money directly to your school account.

Under certain circumstances, loans can be deferred, postponed, canceled or considered for forbearance.

PLUS Loans

PLUS loans are not based on financial need so you may use them to cover your expected family contribution. In fact, creditworthy parents may borrow an amount equal to the student's total cost of attendance less any aid received.

If a parent is judged not to be credit worthy, the student may borrow an additional amount under the unsubsidized Stafford; freshmen and sophomores get an extra $4,000; juniors and seniors, an extra $5,000 (these amounts correspond to the higher borrowing limits for an independent undergraduate).

Loan Origination Fee and Insurance Fees. Lenders may subtract a 3% loan origination fee and a 1% insurance fee. As an extra incentive to borrow from them, lenders may soon be allowed to pay your origination fee. If your loan comes from Uncle, you pay a combined 4% instead. No deals.

Interest Rate. The rate is adjusted annually to equal 3.1% more than the bond equivalent of the 52-week T-bill and carries a 9% cap. Currently, it is 8.72%.

Interest Subsidy. There is no interest subsidy to borrowers.

Repayment begins within 60 days of taking out the loan and extends from 5 to 10 years. Repayment can be deferred while the student is in school; interest, however, continues to accrue.

Who Makes Loans? Private lenders—Banks, S&Ls, Credit Unions, some states, and Uncle Sam (for students attending schools participating in Direct Lending).

Application procedures are similar to Stafford Loans.

Under certain conditions, loans can be deferred, postponed or canceled.

The Direct Lending Debate

So why are there two different programs? The Administration argues the loan process would run more smoothly and at less expense by eliminating the middlemen. Right now, there are thousands of lenders making loans, nearly a hundred secondary markets buying up the loans, dozens of guaranteeing agencies administering loans, and finally, Uncle Sam insuring and subsidizing the whole cycle. Under Direct Lending, there are no middlemen. Uncle is the only lender, wiring money straight to the colleges. Students then repay the Treasury directly.

While many agree the loan process might be simpler with Uncle as the sole lender, there is no guarantee that turning the Department into one of the country's largest banks wouldn't spawn a clumsy and expensive bureaucracy to keep tabs on the $100 billion or so in outstanding loans. Also, the Education Department does not have the (profit) motive of the private sector; a motive that usually contributes to efficiently run, quality programs and lets students shop around for the "best deal." In fact, the threat of direct lending has already brought the private lending community together to improve delivery systems and introduce more creative (less costly) repayment options. In fact, many schools have opted not to participate in direct lending, because their students are getting lower-cost loans from the banking community.

The fate of the program probably hinges on the November elections and the 1997/98 reauthorization of the Higher Education Act. In the meantime, to learn whether your school participates in direct lending contact your financial aid office.

SUPPLEMENTAL EDUCATIONAL OPPORTUNITY GRANTS

Uncle will give the colleges $583 million for SEOGs next year.

Size of awards. From $100 to $4,000 per year of undergraduate study.

Criteria for Selection. Need and availability of funds. Be smart. Apply early. Nearly 1 million SEOG recipients each year; priority goes to those receiving Pells.

WORK-STUDY

Uncle will give the colleges about $685 million for work-study next year.

Eligibility. About 713,000 participants each year, both undergraduate and graduate students. President Clinton would like to see this number increase to one million by the year 2000, as work-study students are more likely to stay in school and graduate with substantially less debt.

Criteria for Selection. Need and availability of funds.

Program Description. On- and off-campus employment. Salary must be at least equal to minimum wage. You cannot earn more money than your award stipulates. Thus, if you receive a $1,000 award, your employment lasts until you earn $1,000 and then it is terminated for that academic year. Employment may not involve any political or religious activity nor may students be used to replace regular employees. Schools must use 5% of their funds for community service projects (this requirement may be waived for select schools).

While we're very happy about the proposed increase in minimum wage, unless more work-study money is appropriated, this program will soon benefit many fewer students. Be smart. Apply early.

PERKINS LOANS

The college acts as lender, using funds originally provided by the federal government. Uncle adds about $160 million per year, and there is now $1 billion in "revolving fund" capital (money paid back by borrowers). Last year, about 725,000 students received an average of $1,342 each.

Eligibility. Undergraduate and graduate students.

Criteria for Selection. Need and availability of funds. Be smart. Apply early.

Loan Limits: $3,000 per year for undergraduates to a maximum of $15,000; $5,000 per year for graduate study to a maximum of $30,000 (less any Perkins money borrowed as an undergraduate). At schools participating in Uncle's *Expanded Lending Option* (to participate, schools must first have default rates under 7.5%), undergraduate students may borrow up to $4,000 per year to a maximum of $20,000; graduate students may borrow up to $6,000 per year to a maximum of $40,000 (less any Perkins money borrowed as an undergraduate).

Minimum Annual Repayment. $480.

Interest rate. 5%.

Interest Subsidy. Student pays no interest while in school or during a 9-month grace period following graduation.

Repayment. 10 years. You may repay via electronic bank transfers. Also, under some circumstances, loans can be deferred, postponed, forgiven, or cancelled.

ON DEFAULTING

Uncle Sam rewards and punishes colleges for their ability to collect on loans. Schools with small default rates (under 7.5%) get an increased infusion of Perkins capital; schools with high default rates (25% +) for three years running may become ineligible for federal funds altogether. (No Perkins money. No Stafford money. No Pell money. No any kind of federal student aid money.) The national default rate is currently about 13% per year (generally lower at four-year schools and higher at trade schools). It may pay you to ask schools for their default rate before you apply.

Uncle Sam can also punish you if you are one of the defaulters, as he should, since in our book, defaulters eclipse even the most parasitic protozoa! He can notify credit bureaus which will damage your credit rating. He can withhold your tax refunds until your loan is repaid. Or, he can garnish your wages (and fine your employer if he/she doesn't follow through). As Uncle gets tougher, the default problem gets better, but at some trade schools defaults still run as high as 85%.

LOAN REPAYMENT OPTIONS

Borrowers with multiple federal loans or borrowers who face larger monthly payments than they can handle under standard, ten-year plans, may want to consolidate their loans and/or use a longer-term repayment plan. Married couples may consolidate their individual loans if they agree to be jointly liable for repayment even if there's a future change in their marital status. Again, Uncle is running two parallel programs, which we'll call regular consolidation and direct consolidation. Under all of these plans, your monthly payments will be smaller but the total amount you repay much greater than under regular (10-year) repayment. For more information, check with Uncle Sam or the institution that gave you your loan.

Extended Repayment

Repayment may extend for 10 years for students with less than $7,500 in loans; 12 years for students with between $7,500 and $10,000 in loans; 15 years for students with between $10,000 and $20,000; 20 years for students with between $20,000 and $40,000; 25 years for students with between $40,000 and $60,000; and 30 years for those lucky students with more than $60,000 to repay. Under regular consolidation, the interest rate cannot exceed the weighted average of all the loans rounded up to the nearest whole percent. Some lenders charge less than this maximum. Shop around. Under direct consolidation, the interest rate cannot exceed 8.25% for Staffords and 9% for PLUS.

Graduated Repayment

Students repay their loan within the framework described above, but payments start small (when incomes are low), and increase over time (while incomes also rise).

Income-Sensitive Repayment

This option is available only from commercial lenders. Students work with their lender to establish a more flexible repayment schedule than the ones above. Payments may be adjusted annually to reflect current and future earning potential.

Income Contingent Repayment

This option is available only under Direct Consolidation. Uncle Sam has developed a complex formula for determining repayment rates; they vary depending on your income and the size of your loan. For example, a single borrower with an income of $25,000 would begin repaying a $12,500 loan at $117 per month while a borrowerer earning $35,000 would repay that same loan at $137 per month. After 25 years, a borrower who has been repaying faithfully, but has not yet retired the loan, will have the rest of his or her debt forgiven. On the down-side, the IRS will count your forgiven loan as in-kind (and taxable) income. Also, students opting for this payment option might wind up paying thousands more in interest than their counterparts who choose one of the other repayment options. Finally, PLUS loans may not be repaid using the Income Contingent option.

ROBERT C. BYRD HONORS SCHOLARSHIPS

No-need, renewable awards of $1,500 intended to promote student excellence. Each state establishes its own criteria and selects recipients.

AMERICORPS

Participants receive a minimum wage stipend and a $4,725 credit per year of full-time service (for a maximum of two years). They may use the credit at any college or graduate school, or to pay down outstanding student loans. Furthermore, the money does not affect their eligibility for other federal student aid. Currently, 23,000 students serve in 350 different programs with Uncle Sam providing most of the funding, but states and nonprofits doing the hiring. Prime projects are those that address unmet needs in education (assisting teachers in Head Start), the environment (recycling or conservation projects), human services (building housing for the homeless) or public safety (leading drug education seminars). Interested students should apply directly to a funded program (for a list, call AmeriCorps, 800-94-ACORPS). Chapter 15 describes some that are already up and running.

While AmeriCorps is small in scope, its real importance has been to focus attention on all the service programs that have emerged in the past decade. With AmeriCorps adding new structure, and a solid core of workers, these programs have become a magnet for corporate "do good" money as well as for volunteers with only an hour to spare. The funded projects have brought huge economic benefits to the communities in which they operate as well as a heightened sense of personal and social responsibility for the AmeriCorps participants. Unfortunately, Congressional critics want to snuff out AmeriCorps saying the government has no business creating a Department of Good Deeds (this year, they voted to take away AmeriCorps money and use it to fund veterans' prosthetic research). Ultimately the battle over AmeriCorps is not about legitimate differences in political philosophy. It's the President's pet program, and an easy target for his opponents.

LOOKING TOWARD REAUTHORIZATION

The Higher Education Act that authorizes all these programs expires in September, 1997. Since no real work will be done until after the November elections, chances are Congress will approve a one year extension and unveil new regulations in 1998. Here are some items being considered: Use tax incentives to encourage families and businesses to save and spend on college. Require schools to provide a greater share of SEOG and Work-Study funds. Collapse all loan programs into one; make the source of funds transparent to the student and let the schools participate in the programs of their choice. Frontload Pell, doubling the size of grants, but limiting them to first and second year students. Exclude trade schools from Pell, and move programs for trade school students to the Labor Department.

America's HOPE Scholarships

President Clinton calls education the "Continental Divide" between those who will prosper economically and those who will not. Unfortunately, many families feel priced out of college. To address this growing problem, he has proposed America's Hope Scholarships. Families with incomes under $100,000 could choose between a tax credit or a tax deduction, whichever would save them more.

The tax-credit would be for $1,500 per full-time student for each of two years (to receive credit in Year Two, students would need a "B" grade average). Families that pay less than $1,500 in taxes would receive a rebate from the Treasury.

The tax deduction would allow families to write off up to $10,000 of income per year, regardless of how many students were in school.

Good politics or good policy? Some call this plan a hastily-assembled-election-year gimmick. And in truth, it's been languishing in Congress with no pressure for action. If, however, Democrats win in November, they've promised to make these incentives a priority.

Chapter 11
The States

All states maintain extensive programs of grants, tuition assistance, fee reductions and loans. About 1.7 million students receive over $2.5 billion in need-based state aid and 250,000 share in $400 million of non-need-based aid.

States making over 50,000 awards: New York, Pennsylvania, Illinois, Ohio, California, Minnesota, Michigan, New Jersey, and Wisconsin —in that order.

States spending over $50 million on student aid: New York, Illinois, California, Pennsylvania, New Jersey, Ohio, Georgia, Florida, Minnesota, Michigan, Virginia, Washington, Massachusetts, Indiana and Wisconsin—in that order.

States where tuition is most affordable when measured against median family income are: Arizona, California, Hawaii, Nevada, North Carolina, and Texas.

States which give money to at least 25% of their students: Georgia, New York, Minnesota, New Jersey, Vermont, Ohio, New Mexico, Pennsylvania, Illinois, Wisconsin, Maine, Colorado, Washington, Massachusetts, Kentucky, Virginia.

ELIGIBILITY FOR STATE-BASED STUDENT AID

States determine eligibility for need-based aid in one of four ways: (1) Twenty-six states use only the federal methodology; (2) Fifteen states use the federal methodology for most of their grants and a hybrid methodology for a few other programs; (3) Two states let schools make the decisions regarding eligibility (South Dakota and Illinois); and (4) Seven states rely on their own system—Louisiana, New York, Ohio, Oklahoma, Oregon, Pennsylvania, and South Carolina.

So, how do you find out which forms to file? In almost all instances, to be considered eligible for state-based student aid, you must file Uncle Sam's FAFSA (and on it, indicate your home state). Some states, those that use the institutional methodology, might ask you to use the College Board's PROFILE, and finally, some states have their own applications. Important: Many states have already noted that using the federal methodology to determine eligibility means more students are qualifying for aid. Unfortunately, state grants are not usually entitlement programs, so when the money runs out, too bad! Again, apply early!

A SUMMARY OF STATE PROGRAMS

The following summary table describes state programs other than state participation in federal programs like the Stafford and PLUS loans. With regard to Stafford and PLUS loans, most states have a guaranteeing agency to administer loans. Their addresses are in *Loans and Grants from Uncle Sam* (inside back cover)

Here is an explanation of the table's columns.

Column 1—In-State Study. These are need-based grants, generally restricted to undergraduates. In the past, most of these grants were funded with help from Uncle Sam's State Student Incentive Grant (SSIG). Unfortunately, SSIG is another target of over zealous budget cutters who feel state grant programs are now well established and no longer need matching funds from Uncle Sam for survival. While it's true that NY, NJ, MN, PA, VT, IL, IA, IN and WA rely on SSIG for less than

2% of their need-based awards, in a dozen other states, SSIG accounts for more than 35% of the total need-based grant budget. Some of these states say that without federal matches they may end their grant programs and transfer the money into other efforts. Funding for 1997/98 does not look promising, so while state grants are not likely to disappear entirely, they will certainly diminish in number. Applying early is more important than ever.

Column 2—Some Other States. These are also need-based grant programs, generally restricted to undergraduates, but these states have signed reciprocity agreements with one or more other states.

Column 3—Merit Programs. Generally, there are three kinds of merit programs. The first type is based on financial need; however, you must meet some academic threshold to be eligible. The second is based on academic accomplishment, but you must demonstrate financial need to qualify for a monetary award, otherwise, your recognition is honorary. The last is based solely on academic accomplishment. Your award is not affected by your finances. Funding for merit-based programs is growing much faster than funding for need-based programs because states don't want to lose their best students to other states.

Column 4—Special Loans. These loans are separate from any federal programs. For example, in Minnesota, first and second year may borrow $4,500 per year at .75% above the 91 day T-bill rate (Juniors and Seniors may borrow $6,000 per year). For all these plans, the loan money is usually secured through tax-exempt bonds issued by the state. In some cases, out-of-state students attending a school in the state underwriting the loans may benefit from the low rates.

Column 5—Teaching. To increase the supply of teachers, many states have instituted special loan programs, with "forgiveness" features if the students actually end up in classrooms. If the students don't go into teaching, they must repay the aid. Some programs limit their benefits to students who teach in a shortage area. This could mean a subject area like math or science. It could also mean a geographic area like rural America or the inner-city.

Column 6—Special Fields. This category covers a variety of programs designed to increase representation in other fields in which the state believes it has shortages. These fields may include medicine, nursing, special education, bilingual education, etc. Many graduate programs are included in this category.

Column 7—Minority Group Programs. The beneficiaries must usually be African-American, Latino or Native American (Eskimo, Indian, or Aleutian).

Column 8—Work-Study. State operated programs similar to the federal work-study or cooperative education programs.

Column 9—Veterans. Special state benefits to state residents who served in the Armed Forces, usually during times of hostilities.

Column 10—National Guard. State educational benefits for serving in the state's National Guard. These are in addition to federal benefits.

Columns 11,12, 13. Special benefits to state residents who are dependents of deceased or disabled veterans, POWs, MIAs, or police/firefighters killed on duty.

Column 14—Military Dependents. These states let military personnel and dependents stationed within the state, attend in-state universities at in-state rates.

Column 15—Tuition Savings Plans. These states operate plans (or have legislation pending) that encourage early planning for college, either "Baccalaureate Bonds," the income from which is tax exempt if used to pay college expenses, or "Prepaid Tuition Plans" in which parents can guarantee tuition at any of the state's public (or in some cases, private) colleges by making a lump sum investment or periodic payments. Prepaid Tuition Plans are also discussed in Chapter 8.

	1. In-State Study	2. Some Other States	3. Merit Programs	4. Special Loans	5. Teaching	6. Special Fields	7. Minority Gp Prgrms	8. Work Study	9. Veterans	10. National Guard	11. Disabled Vet	12. POW or MIA	13. Police/Fireman	14. Active Duty	15. Tuition Savings Plan
											Dependent of	Dependent of	Dependent of		
Alabama	X				X	X	X			X	X		X	X	X
Alaska	X	X	X	X		X	X			X		X		X	X
Arizona	X													X	
Arkansas	X		X		X	X	X			X		X	X	X	
California	X		X		X				X				X	X	X
Colorado	X		X			X	X						X	X	X
Connecticut	X	X	X	X				X	X		X	X	X		
Delaware	X	X	X		X	X		X			X	X	X		
DC	X	X				X	X	X			X	X		X	X
Florida	X				X	X	X	X			X	X		X	X
Georgia	X		X			X	X							X	
Guam		X	X		X	X	X							X	
Hawaii	X		X		X					X					
Idaho	X					X	X	X				X	X	X	
Illinois	X		X			X	X	X	X	X		X	X	X	X
Indiana	X		X			X	X	X							X
Iowa	X		X					X							
Kansas	X		X			X	X	X							
Kentucky	X					X	X	X			X		X	X	X
Louisiana	X		X			X		X		X	X		X	X	
Maine	X	X			X	X	X		X		X	X	X	X	X
Maryland	X	X	X		X	X					X	X	X	X	X
Massachusetts	X	X		X				X	X	X	X	X	X		X
Michigan	X			X				X	X	X	X	X		X	X
Minnesota	X			X		X	X	X			X	X	X	X	
Mississippi	X		X			X	X			X	X	X	X	X	X
Missouri	X		X			X				X	X	X	X	X	X
Montana	X					X	X	X	X		X	X	X	X	
Nebraska	X		X			X	X	X	X	X	X	X	X		
Nevada	X			X		X	X	X	X	X	X	X	X		
New Hampshire	X	X			X						X			X	
New Jersey	X		X	X									X		
New Mexico	X		X			X	X	X	X				X		
New York	X		X	X		X	X	X			X	X	X		X
North Carolina	X		X			X	X	X	X	X	X	X		X	X
North Dakota	X		X			X	X			X	X	X	X	X	X
Ohio	X	X	X			X					X	X	X	X	X
Oklahoma	X		X			X	X						X		X
Oregon	X					X	X				X		X		X
Pennsylvania	X	X				X			X	X			X		X
Puerto Rico	X		X					X		X				X	
Rhode Island	X	X	X	X				X		X	X			X	X
South Carolina			X	X	X	X	X	X		X	X		X	X	X
South Dakota	X		X					X			X	X		X	
Tennessee	X		X		X			X					X		X

85

| | 1. In-State Study | 2. Some Other States | 3. Merit Programs | 4. Special Loans | 5. Teaching | 6. Special Fields | 7. Minority Gp prgrms | 8. Work Study | 9. Veterans | 10. National Guard | Dependent of | | | 14. Active Duty | 15. Tuition Savings Plan |
											11. Disabled Vet	12. POW or MIA	13. Police/Fireman		
Texas	X	X	X			X	X	X	X	X		X	X	X	X
Utah	X						X							X	
Vermont	X	X									X				
Virgin Islands	X					X				X					
Virginia	X		X	X		X		X			X		X		X
Washington	X		X			X	X	X	X		X	X	X	X	
West Virginia	X	X	X		X	X								X	
Wisconsin	X		X			X	X		X	X	X				
Wyoming			X		X	X				X					X

No two states have the same programs. Here are some you should ask about. Your questions might lead you to little-known or special opportunities.

Reciprocal Arrangements I. Reciprocal arrangements between states often permit students living near a state's border to study in the adjoining state at discounted tuition rates. Sometimes this means students pay less by going out-of-state than if they stayed at home. Other times, students pay the same amount whether they go out-of-state or stay home. Unfortunately, these kinds of "trade imbalances" when combined with ever tightening state budgets are causing some states (especially those that take in more students than they send away) to rethink the finances of reciprocity and scale back on their agreements.

Reciprocal Arrangements II. Study out of state at reduced rates when your desired major is not offered in state. Such arrangements are coordinated by consortia such as WICHE (PO Box 9752, Boulder, CO 80301, http://www.wiche.edu) which covers western states; the Southern Regional Education Board (592 10th Street, NW, Atlanta, GA 30318) which operates in the South; and the New England Regional Student Program administered by the New England Board of Education (45 Temple Place, Boston, MA 02111). The Midwest Student Exchange Program can be contacted via state agencies in the Midwest.

Reciprocal Arrangements III. WICHE offers a second program in which students pay reduced tuition at any of the state schools in the region. The reduced rate equals resident tuition plus 50%; a large savings over non-resident rates.

Tuition Equalization. These programs reduce the difference in tuition costs between in-state public and private colleges. Examples: Alabama, Florida, Georgia, Indiana, Iowa, Kansas, Kentucky, New Mexico, North Carolina, Ohio, South Carolina, South Dakota, Texas, Virginia and Wisconsin. These states make grants worth well over $100 million, although the states which face insufficient funds for public schools might start rethinking giving tax money to private schools.

Grant Programs I. Most states provide special assistance to students attending private colleges in state. For example: North Carolina residents who choose an in-state private college receive an automatic (non-need based) $1,150 grant.

Grant Programs II. Some states provide need-based assistance to residents attending schools out-of-state. Alaska, Delaware, Maine, Maryland, Massachusetts, New Hampshire, Ohio, Pennsylvania, Rhode Island, Vermont, West Virginia, and Wisconsin make grants worth $14.5 million.

Free Scholarship Search. Alabama, Florida, Idaho, Illinois, Maine and Vermont offer state residents (free) searches of potential financial aid sources.

Discounts for Senior Citizens. Most of our states give tuition discounts to seniors. Some states waive tuition entirely. See Chapter 23 for more information.

Virtual University. Ten governors (from Arizona, Colorado, Idaho, Nevada, New Mexico, North Dakota, Oregon, Utah, Washington, Wyoming) discussed pooling their resources to create a Virtual University made up of professors throughout the region. They don't intend for this university to replace the traditional college experience, but to serve the needs of non-traditional students.

Community College Partnerships. Many states encourage partnerships between two- and four-year colleges to help make the transition seamless and broaden educational access. Sometimes students are guaranteed admission to the four-year school. Sometimes they're offered additional aid opportunities. And sometimes they are just given guidance on course selection. For example, Arizona, California, Colorado, Connecticut, Delaware, Florida, Illinois, Iowa, Kansas, Kentucky, Maryland, Massachusetts, Minnesota, Mississippi, Montana, New Mexico, North Carolina, Ohio, South Carolina, Tennessee, Virginia, West Virginia and Wyoming.

Community Service Programs. States were way ahead of the community service bandwagon. All fifty now have ties to AmeriCorps, while others also fund their own projects. To find your State Commission on National Service and receive a list of funded programs, contact AmeriCorps, 202/606-5000, 1201 New York Ave. NW, Washington, DC 20525, http://www.cns.gov. If funding for AmeriCorps gets cut (see Chapter 10), expect these programs to shrink, but not disappear.

INNOVATIVE STATE PROGRAMS

Be on the lookout for these. There's lots of action on the state level—some of which will result in important new programs (and some which will fizzle).

Louisiana. START Smart (Student Tuition Assistance and Revenue Trust) is an innovative approach to rewarding early savings for college. Participants save at their own pace and their money is professionally managed by the State Treasurer. The state then adds an annual incentive ranging from 4% to 14% of the amount deposited during the calendar year. For lower income depositors, those with AGIs under $15,000, that match would be at 14%. For higher income depositors, those with AGIs between $75,000 and $100,000, that match would be at 4%.

Georgia: Helping Outstanding Pupils Educationally (HOPE) ensures that every qualified (3.0 GPA or better) Georgia HS grad will receive free tuition at one of Georgia's public colleges or universities, or up to $3,000 for a private, in-state school. Students must maintain a 3.0 GPA while in college to continue receiving money. Nearly 200,000 students have benefitted from this program, which is funded by the Lottery for Education. Contact (in Georgia), 800-546-HOPE.

Michigan: Tuition Incentive Program (TIP). Low income students can get free tuition at community colleges. Those who complete community college are eligible for a $2,000 voucher for use at any of Michigan's four year colleges.

Maine. Education Network of Maine televises courses throughout the state at nearly 80 regional centers and high school sites. Students can request library materials via their computers, and speak with professors via toll free numbers.

Massachusetts: MassPlan allows parents to borrow up to the full amount of college (less any aid received) at a fixed rate of 7.65% with repayment spread over 15 years. This loan is available at 63 participating Massachusetts colleges, to all students regardless of their state of residence. For an extra $300 parents can take advantage of the Home Equity Option. By securing the loan with home equity, interest payments become tax deductible making the after-tax rate equal to 5.28% for someone in the 31% bracket.

Massachusetts: UPlan is a hybrid of many other states' college savings plans. Both residents and nonresidents may invest in Massachusetts bonds and redeem them later for a guaranteed percentage of tuition at any of 70 participating (public and private) Massachusetts colleges. Assume for example the parent buys a $5,000 bond. If tuition this year at State U. is $5,000 and tuition at Private U. is $20,000, that bond will be worth 100% of tuition at State U. or 25% at Private U. regardless of the cost of these two schools when the student eventually enrolls. Massachusetts has promised participating colleges they will be paid a rate equal to the bond's original value plus interest equal to 2% over inflation, compounded annually. The beauty of this plan is not only the peace of mind it gives investors that their savings will keep pace with tuition increases, but also the incentive it gives colleges to keep tuition increases at or below inflation plus 2%. Because Massachusetts invests the money in state-issued bonds, income from the bonds is exempt from state taxes, even if the money is not used for tuition. Investors who decide not to use the money for tuition receive a return equal to their original principal compounded by a rate equal to the CPI. As with most tuition future plans, smart investors can do better on their own (without limiting their college choices), however, for some families, peace of mind is worth this sacrifice.

For more information on MassPlan or UPlan, visit http://www.mefa.org

Arkansas, Louisiana, and Indiana: In Arkansas, they're called Academic Challenge Scholarships. In Indiana, they're called Twenty-First Century Scholars. They have similar themes: States guarantee to pay in-state tuition for low-income students who make certain commitments. For example, students must maintain a specified GPA in college prep courses and remain drug free. This performance-based tuition waiver for at-risk students has been nicknamed "The Taylor Plan" after Patrick Taylor, a Louisiana oil man who realized that many people drop out of HS because they perceive it as a dead end. He figured if you promised at-risk students a college education (assuming they stayed out of trouble and met admission standards), you'd see a huge increase in educational achievement.

Maine. Maine residents attending out-of-state schools, and out-of-state students attending Maine schools can take out a "Super Loan" at 1% below the current Stafford rate. The program is available through 39 participating lenders.

Arizona. To encourage "geography bound" students to pursue four-year degrees, Arizona is experimenting with a plan that would give students money to use at under-utilized private colleges that are nearer to their homes than any of the state's public schools. This alternative is cheaper than building new public university facilities, and will help the state deal with its expected enrollment boom.

Virginia and Texas: Special incentive grants to induce students of one racial group to attend a state public university in which another racial group makes up a significant proportion of the student body.

Colorado, Florida and Minnesota: Public high school students may take courses at no charge at any (public) college in the state that will admit them Students receive both high school and college credit for their work.

DIRECTORY OF STATE AGENCIES

Many state higher education agencies sport virtual addresses where you'll find information on state student aid, links to state schools, research data, news releases, even staff bios. We've underlined the state agencies currently on-line; Uncle will link you up. (http://www.ed.gov/offices/OPE/agencies.html).

Alabama
334-281-1928
AL Commission on Higher Ed.
3465 Norman Bridge Road
Montgomery, AL 36105-2310

Alaska
907-465-2962
Commission on Postsecondary Ed.
3030 Vintage Blvd.
Juneau, AK 99801

Arizona
602-229-2531
Commission for Postsecondary Ed.
2020 N. Central Avenue, #275
Phoenix, AZ 85004

Arkansas
501-324-9300
Department of Higher Education
114 E. Capitol St.
Little Rock, AR 72201

California
916-445-7933
Postsecondary Ed. Commission
1303 J. Street, #500
Sacramento, CA 95814

Colorado
303-866-2723
Commission on Higher Education
1300 Broadway, 2nd Floor
Denver, CO 80203

Connecticut
203-566-2618
Department of Higher Education
61 Woodland Street
Hartford, CT 06105

Delaware
302-577-3240
Higher Education Commission
820 N. French Street
Wilmington, DE 19801

District of Columbia
202-727-3685
DC Office of Postsecondary Ed.
2100 ML King Jr. Ave., SE
Washington, DC 20020

Florida
904-487-0649
Office of Student Fin. Assistance
1344 Florida Education Center
Tallahassee, FL 32399

Georgia
404-414-3000
GA Student Finance Authority
2082 East Exchange Place, #245
Tucker, GA 30084

Hawaii
808-956-8213
Postsecondary Ed Commission
Bachman Hall, Room 202
2444 Dole Street
Honolulu, HI 96822

Idaho
208-334-2270
State Board of Education
PO Box 83720
Boise, ID 83720

Illinois
217-782-6767
State Board of Higher Education
500 West Monroe St., 3rd fl.
Springfield, IL 62704

Indiana
317-232-2350
State Student Assistance Comm.
150 West Market St., 5th floor
Indianapolis, IN 46204

Iowa
515-242-6703, 800-383-4222
Iowa College Aid Commission
200 10th St., 4th fl.
Des Moines, IA 50309

Kansas
913-296-3517
Board of Regents,
700 SW Harrison, #1410
Topeka, KS 66603

Kentucky
502-564-7990, 800-928-8926
Higher Ed. Assistance Auth.
1050 US 127 South
Frankfort, KY 40601-4323

Louisiana
504-922-1011, 800-259-5626
Student Fin. Assistance Comm.
PO Box 91202
Baton Rouge, LA 70821-9202

Maine
207-287-3263
Finance Authority of Maine
PO Box 949
Augusta, ME 04330

Maryland
410-974-5370
MD Higher Ed. Commission
16 Francis Street
Annapolis, MD 21401

Massachusetts
617-727-9420
Higher Ed. Coord. Council
330 Stuart Street
Boston, MA 02116

Michigan
517-373-3394
Higher Ed Assistance Authority
PO Box 30462
Lansing, MI 48909

Minnesota
612-296-3974, 800-657-3866
Higher Ed. Coord. Board
550 Cedar Street, #400
St. Paul, MN 55101

Mississippi
601-982-6663
Financial Assistance Board
3825 Ridgewood Road
Jackson, MS 39211-6453

Missouri
314-751-2361
Coord. Board for Higher Ed.
3515 Amazonas Drive
Jefferson City, MO 65109

Montana
406-444-6594
MT University System
2500 Broadway
Helena, MT 59620

Nebraska
Postsecondary Ed. Coord. Bd.
PO Box 95005
Lincoln, NE 68509

Nevada
702-687-5915
State Department of Education
400 W. King St.,
Carson City, NV 89710

New Hampshire
603-271-2555
Postsecondary Ed. Commission
2 Industrial Park Drive
Concord, NH 03301-8512

New Jersey
609-588-3268, 800-792-8670
Office of St. Fin. Assistance
4 Quakerbridge Plaza, CN 540
Trenton, NJ 08625

New Mexico
505-827-7383
Comm. on Higher Education
1068 Cerrillos Road
Santa Fe, NM 87501

New York
518-474-5642
Higher Ed. Services Comm.
One Commerce Plaza
Albany, NY 12255

North Carolina
919-821-4771
State Ed. Assistance Authority
PO Box 2688
Chapel Hill, NC 27515

North Dakota
701-224-4114
Student Financial Asst. Prgm.
600 East Boulevard Ave.
Bismark, ND 58505

Ohio
614-466-7420, 800-837-6752
OH Student Aid Commission
PO Box 182452
Columbus, OH 43218-2452

Oklahoma
405-524-9100
OK State Regents for Higher Ed
PO Box 3020
Oklahoma City, OK 73101

Oregon
503-687-7400
State Scholarship Commission
1500 Valley River Drive, #100
Eugene, OR 97401

Pennsylvania
717-257-2800, 800-692-7435
Higher Ed Assistance Agency
1200 North 7th Street
Harrisburg, PA 17102

Rhode Island
401-277-2050, 800-922-9855
Higher Ed. Assistance Authority
560 Jefferson Boulevard
Warwick, RI 02886

South Carolina
803-737-1200
SC Commission on Higher Ed.
1310 Lady St., #811
Columbia, SC 29201

South Dakota
605-773-3134
Office of the Secretary
Dept. of Education
700 Governors Drive
Pierre, SD 57501-2291

Tennessee
615-741-1346, 800-342-1663
TN Student Assistance Corp.
404 James Robertson Parkway
Parkway Towers, Suite 1950
Nashville, TN 37243-0820

Texas
512-483-6340, 800-242-3062
Higher Ed. Coordinating Board
Box 12788, Capitol Station
Austin, TX 78711

Utah
801-321-7205
Utah State Board of Regents
335 W.N. Temple, 3 Triad, # 550
Salt Lake City, UT 84180-1205

Vermont
802-655-9602, 800-642-3177
Vermont Student Assistance Corp.
Champlain Mill, Box 2000
Winooski, VT 05404

Virginia
804-786-1690
Council of Higher Education
101 North 14th Street
Richmond, VA 23219

Washington
206-753-7850
Higher Ed. Coordinating Board
917 Lake Ridge Way, SW
Olympia, WA 98504

West Virginia
304-588-2691
State Dept. of Education
1900 Washington St., #358
Charleston, WV 25305

Wisconsin
608-267-2206
Higher Educational Aids Board
PO Box 7885
Madison, WI 53707

Wyoming
307-777-6265
State Dept. of Education
2300 Capitol Ave., 2nd fl.
Cheyenne, WY 82002

Part V
The Big Alternatives

OK. You are willing to pick up a little maturity along with your education. You are willing to invest some extra time into earning a baccalaureate. And you want to start your professional career without the staggering burden of student debt. What can you do? You can investigate two major alternative methods of financing an education: (1) Letting the boss pay for it or (2) letting the military pay for it.

Part V covers both of these "employee" tuition plans—those found in Madison Avenue corporate offices and those sponsored by the US Military.

Chapter 12
Letting the Boss Pay for It

COMPANY TUITION AID

Once upon a time you could go to work for a company that had a tuition reimbursement plan, take college courses on your own time, and let the employer foot the bill. Then the IRS decided this was too good a deal. It ruled that courses had to be job-related to qualify as a benefit. Courses not job-related, but paid for by the employer, had to be declared as taxable income. That ruling pulled the rug out from what had promised to become a major alternative program for young people. The reason: Jobs at the bottom are often so narrowly defined that few courses required for a degree could pass the "job-related test." Why would a shipping clerk need a course in American History? While hurting people at the entry level, the law had little impact on the educational pursuits of the higher-ups. A manager might justify a course in English Literature to improve her writing skills and a sales manager could qualify for an Anthropology program to better understand the cultural factors that influence buying.

The Tax-Reform Act of 1986 brought back the exclusion of non job-related tuition benefits (Section 127 for anyone who cares to read the 1.3 million word tax code), but limited the exclusion to $5,250 per year. Since then, Congress has continued to extend the exclusion, but on a year-to-year basis. The exclusion expires every September 30, however, with nearly 3,000 employers offering Section 127 plans, and around 800,000 workers taking advantage of them, we anticipate another extension this year.

Graduate students may no longer be eligible for this exclusion after 1996!

Even if your employer does reimburse you for tuition, and the reimbursement remains a tax-free benefit, there may be strings attached. For example, you may have to stay with the firm for a set number of years after you graduate, or maintain a certain grade point average while in school. These requirements are only fair—after all, employers help employees with their education for the good of the company, not just for the good of the employee. Ford is one company that realizes this; it pays 100% of any course approved by a boss.

Still, a better program for the beginner is Cooperative Education.

COOPERATIVE EDUCATION

Cooperative Education combines formal studies with an off-campus job related to your major. The money earned on the job will, in most cases, cover college costs. In some schools, practically the entire student body participates in cooperative education. Examples: Northeastern University (MA), and GMI Engineering & Management Institute (MI). There are three common methods for rotating between school and work:

- **The alternating method.** Under this method, you are a full-time student for a term or semester, then you work for a term or a semester, with the cycle repeating itself until you graduate—usually in five years.

- **The parallel method.** Here you attend classes part time and work between 15 and 25 hours a week. You may be a student in the morning and a worker in the afternoon, or vice versa. This method, too, may require five years for degree completion.
- **Extended day method.** The student works full-time and attends school in the evening.

Employers like the co-op program, considering it, in the Wall Street Journal's words, "a source of realistic, work-oriented, future full-time employees."

Some statistics about cooperative education: 900 participating colleges, 50,000 participating employers, 200,000 enrolled students who earn $1.3 billion each year. The biggest employer, offering the widest choice of work sites, academic plans and career fields: Uncle Sam (over 18,000 students).

WHAT'S NEW IN COOPERATIVE EDUCATION?

Uncle Sam has consolidated his various work/school programs into a single Student Educational Employment Program (SEEP), which has two components:

The Student Temporary Employment Program which gives students the flexibility to earn a salary while continuing their studies. The work may be during the summer or school year and need not be related to the student's academic field of study.

The Student Career Experience Program which gives students work experience directly related to their field of study. Students alternate formal periods of work and study and may be eligible for permanent employment after graduation.

COOPERATIVE EDUCATION RESOURCES

1. *The Advantages of Cooperative Education* and *Co-op/Career* brochure from the National Commission for Cooperative Education. The first brochure describes the benefits of co-op for students, employers and colleges. The other highlights career benefits from participation in co-op. NCCE, 360 Huntington Avenue, 384CP, Boston, MA 02115; e-mail: ncce@lynx.neu.edu. Also, *Cooperative Education Undergraduate Program Roster.* A list of colleges offering cooperative education, arranged alphabetically by state.
2. *Directory of College Cooperative Education Programs* published by Oryx Press and the Commission for Cooperative Education (see address above).
3. *Earn and Learn: Your Guide to In-School Educational Employment Programs* links you up with federal program—you'll find an overview of federal co-op, the sponsoring agencies, and the participating colleges (inside back cover).
4. *Your Home State.* Nearly half the states have work-study or co-op programs. If your counselor doesn't have your state's Co-op Education Center address, call your state agency (Chapter 11) and ask them for the information.
5. *Your College.* Nearly 900 colleges have cooperative education programs. If the financial aid office doesn't have the information you need, ask if there's a separate co-op office on campus.

INTERNSHIPS

It's hard to draw the line between cooperative education and internships. Two general distinctions: The alternating involvement between formal studies and work, in cooperative education, extends throughout a student's college career, while internships often last only one semester or one summer break. Participants in cooperative education always get a paycheck; interns may or may not. In fact, the more "desirable" the internship, the less the pay.

Chapter 13
Putting on the Uniform

Don't overlook the military as a source of financial aid. You can pick up tuition dollars before you enter the service, while in uniform, and after being discharged. There are programs for active duty personnel and programs for being in the Reserves or the National Guard. And there are programs for officers and programs for enlisted people.

Military tuition benefits are dispensed with no reference to financial need. You qualify for them, whether you are rich or poor. But they are not free. The military will want something in return. At a minimum you'll have to get a haircut, salute superior officers and give a few years of your time. The U.S. Armed Forces have collaborated on a web site that will link you up with lots of options, and answer your questions (oh-so-objectively), about whether the military is for you, http://myfuture.com (or 800/893-LEAD)

Service Status	Typical Programs
Before Entering Service	Military Academies ROTC Medical Programs One-Shot Programs
In Service	Commissioned Officers Off-Duty Programs Reserve Duty Programs Loan Forgiveness Options
After Service	Montgomery GI Bill Dependent Benefits Benefits for Former Military

BEFORE ENTERING SERVICE

Military Academies

The academies are extremely competitive. Good grades, extracurricular activities, leadership and athletic excellence are in demand. So are superb health and solid SAT scores. You should have 600+ on the math portion and combined scores of 1200 or more. Contact the academies during your junior year of high school. Most appointments are made by Representatives and Senators. Tell your elected officials about your interest. Make sure they open a file on you in their offices. Keep feeding that file with your achievements. Also add recommendations. Make sure you obtain recommendations from people who are deemed important by the elected officials.

ROTC Scholarships

The military has one-, two- and four-year ROTC scholarships. These scholarships will pay for tuition, books and fees. You will also get a small monthly allowance or a flat stipend (e.g., $1,000 per year). The Army offers its scholarships at three levels regardless of actual tuition costs: $12,800, $9,000 or $5,000 per year. In addition, each scholarship winner receives $450 per year for books and supplies and up to $1,500 per year in (tax free) spending money.

A 1250 SAT (28 ACT) will enhance your chances for an ROTC scholarship. So will a varsity letter and membership in the National Honor Society. Nearly all scholarship winners are in the top 25% of their HS class; Three-quarters are class officers, and over 55% are captains of varsity athletic teams. Application should be made by November 1 of your senior year (the Army has an early application option with a July 15 deadline). There will probably be an interview. Before the interview, brush up on current events. Also, be prepared to give your reasons for seeking a military career. An interest in the physical sciences, engineering or nursing will help.

ROTC is not offered at all colleges. The services will provide you with a list. You may use your award at any college on that list assuming you are able to secure admission (something you must do on your own).

The Regular ROTC Program

This is not a scholarship program. Students join the program in their freshman year, at colleges that offer ROTC. For two years they march and salute for free. In their junior and senior years, participants do get paid: $100 per month.

ROTC-Coop Education Combination

The Army reserves cooperative education positions for some ROTC cadets in nearby Army installations. These positions, which provide added earnings, will also lead to federal employment after the participant has served on active duty.

Military Medical Programs

See Chapter 20

One-Shot Programs

On occasion, the Navy and the Air Force need highly specialized technical people and will use financial aid as a recruiting tool. For instance, the Air Force has a "College Senior Engineer Program" for students in electrical, nuclear, astronautical and aeronautical engineering. Students can sign up during their junior year. In their senior year, they will receive $1740 or $900 per month. After graduation, they are called to active duty, attend Officer Training School and serve as a commissioned officer.

MORE INFORMATION

ROTC:

Army ROTC
800-USA-ROTC

Marine Corps
800-MARINES

Navy ROTC
800-USA-NAVY

Air Force ROTC
800-423-USAF

ACADEMIES:

Admissions Office, USMA
606 Thayer Road
West Point, NY 10996
800/822-USMA
http://www.usma.edu

Director of Cadet Admissions
USAF Academy
Colorado Springs, CO 80840
800/443-9266
http://www.usafa.af.mil

Admissions
US Merchant Marine Academy
Kings Point, NY 11024
http://www.usmma.edu

Candidate Guidance
US Naval Academy
Leahy Hall
Annapolis, MD 21402
800/638-9156
http://www.nadn.navy.mil

Admissions
US Coast Guard Academy
15 Mohegan Avenue
New London, CT 06320
http://www.dot.gov/dotinfo/uscg

IN SERVICE EDUCATIONAL BENEFITS

Commissioned Officer

Each year, the services select hundreds of officers to attend graduate schools. The chosen officers receive full pay and allowances and have all their educational expenses met while pursuing their master's degree or doctorate.

Off-Duty Programs

All services have arrangements with civilian colleges and encourage off-duty course work, with the services paying up to 75% of the tuition costs (amount varies with rank and length of service). Through credit transfers and arrangements with accrediting institutions, such off-duty courses can be accumulated to gain credit for associate, baccalaureate or even master's degrees. For more information on this and the 1000 schools participating in the Army's Concurrent Admissions Program (CONAP) contact Servicemembers Opportunity Colleges, National Headquarters, One Dupont Circle, Suite 680, Washington DC 20036.

Reserve Duty Programs

Through the National Guard and Army Reserves, you can receive approximately $7,124 in (tax-free) education benefits under the Montgomery GI Bill. That combined with good, part-time pay as a reservist can total $25,100 over six years. Furthermore, you can earn cash bonuses—for example up to $2,000 for enlistment in the reserves or completing advanced training in the National Guard.

Loan Repayment Options

The Army Reserve, National Guard, and the Regular Army also offer repayment on federal student loans (e.g., Stafford and Perkins). In the Army Reserve and National Guard, you may have up to $10,000 forgiven at the rate of 15% or $1,500 per year, whichever is greater. As an incentive for enlistment in selected skills, the Army will double those amounts to $20,000 in total loans, forgiven at the rate of 15% or $3,000 per year, whichever is greater. In the Regular Army you may have up to 1/3 of your loan forgiven per year of active service, to a maximum of $55,000.

AFTER SERVICE BENEFITS

The Montgomery GI Bill

This is a contributory system. While on active duty, the soldier, sailor, or airman allocates $100 per month (to a maximum of $1,200) to an educational fund. At the end of a two-year enlistment, the Veteran's Administration will contribute $10,986; at the end of a four-year enlistment the VA will contribute $13,798. After you leave the military, the money you earned will be paid directly to you in monthly installments for each month you're enrolled in college. For example, if you enlisted for four years and qualified for $14,998 ($13,798 + $1,200), you would receive $416 per month for 36 months to help you pay your educational costs. Since there are generally nine months in a school year, this income stream should cover you for your full four years. You have ten years to use your education benefits from the date of your discharge. Note: This benefit increases each year with the inflation rate.

The Army sweetens the pot with bonuses for enlisting in what it calls critical "Military Occupation Specialties" (MOS). This could add up to $7,813 for a two-year enlistment or $15,002 for a four-year enlistment bringing your total fund to $20,000 or $30,000 respectively. The Army calls this bonus "The Army College Fund." Call 1-800-USA-ARMY for more information. The Navy and Marines Corps have similar benefits. Call your local Service recruiter for more details.

Dependents Education Assistance

Wives and children of veterans who died or were totally disabled as the result of service qualify for Veterans Administration educational benefits. These benefits are also extended to dependents of former Prisoners of War and soldiers classified as MIA—Missing in Action.

State Educational Benefits

Most states have aid programs for Veterans and their dependents. See Chapter 11 and write to your state's Office of Veteran Affairs (addresses in *Need A Lift*).

BENEFITS FOR MILITARY DEPENDENTS

Army

1. Army Emergency Relief. Scholarships for unmarried children of active duty, retired, or deceased soldiers. For scholarships, apply by March 1 to Army Emergency Relief, 200 Stovall Street, Alexandria, VA 22332.
2. Summary of Educational Benefits. Request DA Pamphlet 352-2, Headquarters, Department of the Army TAPC-PDE, Washington, D. C. 20314.

Air Force

Air Force Aid Society. General Henry H. Arnold Education Grant program ($1,000 per grant) for dependent sons and daughters of active duty, retired or deceased Air Force as well as spouses of active duty members (stationed stateside only) attending undergraduate college. Veterans and reservists not eligible. Approximately 5,000 grants per year. Air Force Aid Society, Education Assistance, 1745 Jefferson Davis Highway, Suite 202, Arlington, VA 22202-3410, 800/429-9475. By mid-March.

Navy/Marines

Dependent's Scholarship Program for U.S. Navy, Marine Corps, and Coast Guard Dependents. More than 75 Navy-oriented organizations currently sponsor scholarships or offer aid for study beyond the high school level. Dependent sons and daughters of Navy, Marine Corps, Coast Guard, and former members are eligible for these scholarships or aid. Information may be obtained from *Need A Lift?* (see below)

BENEFITS FOR THE FAMILIES OF FORMER MILITARY

Former military families tend to congregate in organizations after leaving the service. Nearly every military association sponsors student aid programs to the children of its members. For a comprehensive list, obtain the useful annual book *Need a Lift?* published by The American Legion, Emblem Sales, PO Box 1050, Indianapolis, IN 46206, $3.00, prepaid. Here are a few examples:

AMVETS Memorial Scholarship

15 awards of $4,000 each (spread over 4 years). Applicants must be veterans, or the son or daughter of a veteran and must have exhausted all government financial aid. Must also demonstrate need and academic achievement and be a US citizen. Must maintain a 3.0 GPA. Applications available between January 1 and February 15 (due by April 15). Send SASE to AMVETS National Headquarters, attn. Scholarships, 4647 Forbes Blvd., Lanham, MD 20706, 301/459-9600.

Reserve Officer Association

Henry J. Reilly Memorial Scholarships. 100 (merit-based) awards for dependents of Association members; 25 for graduate students, 75 for undergrads. Deadlines vary from April 1 to April 30. For additional eligibility criteria and application request, send SASE to Scholarship Fund, ROA, One Constitution Avenue, NE, Washington, DC 20002.

Retired Officers Scholarship Program

Interest-free loan program for undergraduate students who are dependent children of active, reserve and retired uniformed service personnel. Maximum loan: $10,000 ($2,500 per year) spread over five years. Repayment begins three to four months after leaving college. Recipients of this loan are automatically considered for several TROA sponsored grant programs. Request application by mid-February from Scholarship Committee, TROA, 201 N. Washington St., Alexandria, VA 22314.

A POSSIBLE STRATEGY

Go on active duty for three or four years. While on active duty, take off-duty courses (for which the military will pay up to 75% of the tuition costs) and make sure the courses add up to an associate degree. At the same time participate in the Montgomery GI Bill. When you are ready for discharge, you will have credit for two years of college and a tuition kitty of nearly $15,000 (more if you were in the infantry) to help you pay for the last two years of college. By the time you get your degree, you will be one, or at the most, two years older than your contemporaries who did not go into service. That minor disadvantage will be offset by somewhat greater maturity and self-confidence. Plus, you'll probably be free of debt.

Part VI
Special Opportunities

Chapter 14

Private Sources with Few Strings

Coca-Cola Scholars Foundation, Inc.

151 scholarships per year, 50 for $5000 per year, renewable for up to 4 years. 100 are for $1000 per year, renewable for up to 4 years. Applications available only through high school guidance office. Applicants must be high school seniors. Application must be postmarked on or before October 31. Course of study in any discipline. Merit-based scholarship emphasizing leadership. Write to Coca-Cola Scholars Foundation, PO Box 442, Atlanta, GA 30301-0442, 1-800-306-COKE.

Educational Scholarship Fund

Awards for vision and motivation. $100 to $5000. Essay required. PO Box 2077, Tulsa, OK 91610. By December 15.

Elks National Foundation

Nearly 500 awards, over $2 million awarded. HS senior, US citizen. Scholarship, leadership, and financial need. Application from local Elk Lodge. By mid-January.

Hattie M. Strong Foundation

Interest-free loans for college students within one year of graduation. Up to $3,000 per year. Repayment based on monthly earnings. Applications available between Jan. 1 and March 31 for consideration for the academic year beginning the next September. Hattie M. Strong Foundation, 1620 Eye St., NW, Suite 700, Washington, DC 20006.

Hitachi Foundation

The Yoshiyama Award. Given annually to 6-10 high school seniors. Not a scholarship and not based on academic achievements. Award is in recognition of outstanding community service and is accompanied by a gift of $5,000 over two years with no restrictions as to how gift is to be used. Nominees need not be college-bound. By 1 April to Yoshiyama Award, PO Box 19247, Washington, DC 20036. (202) 457-0588.

Pickett & Hatcher Educational Fund, Inc.

Low interest (6%) loan to full time undergraduates in fields of study *other than* law, medicine, or the ministry. Up to $16,000 total (over 4 years). Loan recipients may not have other educational loans and must be legal residents of and attend four-year colleges in one of the following states: Alabama, Florida, Georgia, Kentucky, Mississippi, North Carolina, South Carolina, Tennessee or Virginia. This fund has helped 19,000 students since 1938. Based on scholastic ability, character, financial need. Request application from Pickett & Hatcher Educational Fund, P.O. Box 8169, Columbus, GA 31908.

Scholarship Contests (miscellaneous)

There are new contests every year! Keep your eyes open and you'll see notices mixed in with your Sunday paper. For example, this year Discover Card is having a $900,000 scholarship contest. Quill Corporation is giving away $200,000.

Chapter 15
Money in Your Community

Nearly every community offers scholarship help to its young citizens. The grants can vary in size from one hundred dollars to several thousand. Community awards are usually circumscribed in their geographic coverage and you must learn about them yourself. There is no central registry. Read the local newspaper carefully, especially the page devoted to club and community affairs. Visit the Chamber of Commerce. It might keep track of business and corporate scholarships offered in your area. Also visit the American Legion Post. The legionnaires take a special interest in helping people with their education. And finally, ask your high school counselor! Here are some examples:

Your City

Examples: Students who graduate from the Cleveland Public Schools can earn $1000 for their first year of college if they meet the following benchmarks: Pass a set of proficiency exams in 8th grade; enroll in core curriculum courses throughout their four years of high school; maintain at least a 2.5 GPA; earn at least a 16 on the ACT (or a combined math/verbal SAT score of 740); and matriculate into a Pell Grant eligible school. To learn more about starting this program in your city (or high school), write, *Gateway to Excellence,* Cleveland Initiative for Education, 2000 E. 9th Street., #808, Cleveland, OH 44115.

Your Community

Look for scholarship bulletins from civic associations, businesses, PTA chapters, social and professional clubs, fraternal organizations, patriotic and veterans organizations. Some communities do very well by their students. For example, journalist Carl Rowan founded "Project Excellence," a program that gives scholarships to some of the Washington DC area's brightest African-American students. This year Mr. Rowan raised nearly $4 million and awarded 108 scholarships (ranging from $4,000 to $60,000). In addition to private donors in your community, you should look toward larger local foundations. There are nearly 400 community funds nationwide which award nearly $100 million to education projects annually!

Your High School

Many high schools have established information clearing houses to work in conjunction with the guidance office. Students (and their parents) may attend workshops on college financing; they receive individual assistance on filing aid applications; they have access to current financial aid literature; and in some instances, they can tap into computerized scholarship data bases. ALL FOR FREE! Some schools have even created foundations to provide "last dollar scholarships" for students with exceptional financial need. Examples: The Scholarship Fund of Alexandria (VA), I Know I Can, Columbus (OH), and California Community Foundation, Los Angeles (CA).

I Have A Dream

Over a decade ago, the very wealthy Eugene Lang promised college scholarships (and extra counseling) to an entire 6th grade class at his former elementary school in East Harlem. In 1986, he created the I Have A Dream Foundation to help other people start similar projects. Reviews have been mixed. Many sponsors have had great success getting at-risk students through HS and into college. Others have found that money alone isn't enough to compensate for missing parents, missing discipline, missing expectations and missing hope. They've learned that a successful program also requires a significant number of volunteers to keep the Dreamers on track. Today, about 10,000 students benefit from over 140 "I Have A Dream" projects in 41 cities across the country. Unfortunately, needy students can't apply directly for this assistance; they can only hope someone will adopt their class (and at a minimum investment of $300,000/class, benefactors are hard to find).

Corporate Generosity

It's still too early to tell whether "I Have a Dream" has been effective, but corporate America is jumping on the bandwagon...witness "The Pepsi Challenge" in which the soft-drink company provided college scholarship money for "at-risk" students at selected high schools in Detroit and Dallas who met certain GPA and attendance requirements. Similarly, *The Washington Post* gives students at Eastern High School in Washington DC $500 for college for each semester they get all A's and B's. More than 100 Post staffers now serve as mentors and more than 30 colleges and universities now offer matching grants. For more information on establishing student incentive programs like The Eastern High School 500 Club, please call Dr. Vincent Reed at (202) 334-6834.

Dollars for Scholars

Dollars for Scholars chapters are community-based, volunteer-operated scholarship foundations affiliated with the *Citizen's Scholarship Foundation of America, Inc.* (CSFA) Dollars for Scholars chapters provide financial assistance, academic support programs, and community support for students seeking postsecondary education. CSFA provides nonprofit status, guidelines and materials for chapter operations. All funds raised locally are distributed by a local awards committee to students of the community. Ask your counselor if your community has a Dollars for Scholars chapter. If not, and you'd like to start one, contact: Dollars for Scholars, PO Box 297, St. Peter, MN 56082, 800-248-8080.

Community Service Programs

The Corporation for National Service wants to continue funding about 20,000 AmeriCorps positions this year, but even if Congressional critics succeed in eliminating this highly and widely praised public service program (see Chapter 10), there will still be opportunities available via your home state or a local agency. These 80+ state and local organizations spend over $131 million annually on conservation and youth-service corps and enable 30,000 additional volunteers to be rewarded for work on education, environmental and public safety programs. While each community is free to run its own program, there are several common threads. In general, corps members work on projects in teams made up of 5-10 people from a wide variety of backgrounds (this racial, ethnic, and economic diversity is at the heart of most programs—everyone benefits from the experiences and perspectives of their fellow participants). In exchange for service, they receive a living allowance (ranging from $100 to $170 per week) and a bonus upon completion of their service commitment. Bonuses range up to $5000 per year of full-time service to a maximum of $10,000. Some programs don't require you to use the bonus for education expenses; others give smaller bonuses to the non-college bound. In general, the higher the stipend, the lower the education bonus. Also, in most programs, workers wear easily identifiable uniforms (e.g., fashionable red t-shirts).

To learn more about your state's community service programs, request a list of State Commission Contacts from the Corporation for National Service (see resources, below). Here are some sample programs:

City Volunteer Corps (New York City). Founded in 1984, this was one of the country's first community-based service programs. Around 750 volunteers each year log countless hours helping the elderly, tutoring children and cleaning up parks. In addition, volunteers who have dropped out of school must complete work for their GED.

City Year (Boston, Chicago, other cities nationwide). City Year is frequently mentioned as a model for a national plan. Boston alone has nearly 500 participants (ages 17-24) who clean parks, organize summer camps, lead day trips, etc. Workers earn $100 per week with a $5,000 bonus at the end of 9-months (the money need not be used for college). Workers are docked for missed days. Before the year is over, workers must register to vote, obtain a library card, produce a resume, learn to prepare their taxes, and get their GED (if not already a graduate). 617/927-2500, http://www.bitgroup.com/development/city_year/

Georgia Peach Corps. The Peach Corps employs about 100 youths, ages 17-25. They work at minimum wage on selected human service and public works projects in rural communities. At the end of one year, they receive $5,000 in credit toward tuition costs at any college nationwide.

Delta Service Corps. The Delta Service Corps places workers age 17+ in existing community organizations across some of the poorest regions of our country (142 counties in Arkansas, Louisiana and Mississippi). Corps members receive a $5,000 education voucher for each of two years of full-time service; $2,000 for each of three years if they're only serving part-time. In January, 1993, the Corps began training its first 270 workers (it soon plans to expand to 1,000).

New Orleans Youth Action Corps volunteers focus on recycling projects, using trash and recyclable materials to create public sculptures and murals. They're also planting trees and plants on city river banks.

Teach for America. Recruits recent college grads to spend two years teaching in understaffed public schools nationwide 212/425-9039.

Public Allies (Chicago, Washington, DC, other cities nationwide). Interns (Allies) between the ages of 18 and 30 receive a stipend ($18,000) plus an education bonus ($5,000). In Chicago, the focus is on housing issues, health care and special needs of at-risk youth. Other cities may differ. Highly competitive program with as many as 35 applicants per position.

Resources
1. *Corporation for National Service.* Ask for the AmeriCorps brochure, list of State Commission Contacts and description of funded programs. 1201 New York Avenue, NW, Washington DC, 20525, 800-94-ACORPS. You can also read program descriptions and get contact information from http://www.cns.gov.
2. *National Association of Service and Conservation Corps.* Publishes a directory of eighty youth service and conservation corps, 666 11th Street NW, Suite 500, Washington DC 20001, 202/737-6272.

Chapter 16
Are Your Parents Eligible?

You may be eligible for financial assistance because your parents were in the military service or presently work for a particular company or belong to a union. A trade group or association can become a source of aid; so can parental membership in patriotic, civic or fraternal associations. Locating these opportunities will require a systematic approach and considerable parental cooperation. The chart below can help organize your search strategy

Eligibility Category	Where to Start Looking
Military Service	*Need A Lift?* $3.00 from The American Legion, Attn: Emblem Sales, PO Box 1050, Indianapolis, IN 46206. Also Chapter 13.
Employment	Personnel Director
Union	*AFL-CIO Guide to Scholarships and Awards.* Free for union members. All others send $3.00 to AFL-CIO Publications Office, 815 16th St., NW, #209, Washington, DC 20006.
Trade Associations	Gale's *Encyclopedia of Associations*
Patriotic/Civil/Fraternal Associations	Gale's *Encyclopedia of Associations*

Here are some samples of the kind of information you will uncover. Remember, these are only a few of the many opportunities.

WHERE DO YOUR PARENTS WORK?

Loans

A growing number of large companies help make it easier for employee children to participate in the Stafford Loan program. The companies put up a reserve against loan defaults, then hire firms like United Student Aid Funds to administer the program and find banks to act as lenders. Ford, General Electric, Texaco, and Time, are among the 150 that provide this service. To find out if your company has such a plan, ask the employee benefits coordinator or call United Student Aid Funds, 1-800-LOAN-USA.

RJR Nabisco goes one better and pays the guarantee fee and subsidizes the interest rate for PLUS loan borrowers.

Scholarships

Many companies sponsor scholarships for employee children as part of their fringe benefit programs.

Merit scholarships. Approximately 2,500 renewable, need-based awards (ranging from $500 to $4,000) sponsored by over 400 corporations for employee children who are Merit Program Finalists (see Chapter 18).

General scholarships for employee children. Sometimes these scholarship programs are designed and managed by non-profit services. The Citizen's Scholarship Fund of America (CSFA), for example, handles programs for about 500 companies, distributing in excess of 20,000 scholarships per year worth about $33 million.

FEEA Fund Scholarships for civilian federal employees and their dependent family members. The 300+ awards (out of 4,700 applications) range from $300 to $1,500. By May 31. Essay required. For an application, send a SASE to the Federal Employee Education and Assistance Fund Scholarship Award, 8441 W. Bowles Ave., Suite 200, Littleton, CO 80123.

Savings Plans

Ask your company's employee benefits coordinator about any special savings programs. More and more employers support and encourage their employees efforts to save for college. Here are some examples:

Contributory Accounts. These work much like retirement accounts with companies matching their employee's contributions. RJR Nabisco, for example, matches employee contributions of up to $4,000 per child.

Educational Savings Plans. Using payroll deductions, employees stash money into a company-managed educational fund. These may be matched, or not, depending on the generosity of the employer. NIKE, for example, matches employee deposits at a ratio of 25 cents for each $1 to a maximum of $1,000.

Free Advice. Some companies don't provide you any extra money, but they will include free or discounted college advice as part of your benefits package. And sometimes good advice is worth more than an extra $500.

ARE YOUR PARENTS MEMBERS OF...

A Trade Group or Association?

Employees of member firms may be eligible. Examples: *National Continental Association of Resolute Employers; National Office Products Association; National Association of Tobacco Distributors.* Addresses in Gale's *Encyclopedia of Associations.*

A Patriotic/Civic/Fraternal Association?

Among many organizations making awards to members and members' children: *Knights of Columbus; International Order of Job's Daughters; United Daughters of the Confederacy;* Yes—even the *Society for the Preservation of Barber Shop Quartets* has sixteen scholarships. Addresses in Gale's *Encyclopedia of Associations.*

A Union?

Examples: AFSCME, American Federation of Teachers, Communications Workers of America, Fire Fighters, Food and Commercial Workers, Teamsters, Letter Carriers, Chemical Workers, Postal Workers, Garment Workers, Hospital & Health Care Employees, Seafarers, Machinists, Mine Workers, Transport Workers, etc. For a list of over $4 million in scholarships, request the *AFL-CIO Guide to Union Sponsored Scholarships, Awards, and Student Financial Aid.* Free to union members. All others should send $3.00 to AFL-CIO Publications and Materials Office, 815 16th Street, NW, Rm. 209, Washington, DC 20006.

Chapter 17
Money from Your Affiliations

Your background, employment record, religion, and nationality as well as your membership in clubs and associations may be the key to financial opportunity. Here, as in the previous chapter, you will have to develop a systematic search strategy. The questions below will get you started.

Question. Does any job I ever held lead to a financial aid award? (Rule out baby-sitting for grouchy Mrs. Grumpelstein). **Answer.** Check with the personnel office of your present or former employers.

Question. What about my future career? Any hope for a scholarship if I become an engineer? **Answer.** See Chapters 20 and 21 for some ideas of what you'll find. Also, search the Web and Gale's *Encyclopedia of Associations* for addresses of professional associations that match your interests.

Question. How about my clubs? **Answer.** Check with chapter/club president or faculty adviser.

Question. What about my religious affiliation? Does my denomination sponsor aid awards? **Answer.** See your minister, priest, or rabbi or write to the national organizations sponsored by the denomination. Addresses in Gale's *Encyclopedia of Associations* in the reference room of the public library.

Question. How about my ancestry or my nationality? **Answer.** Write to the organizations serving your ancestry or your nationality. Addresses in Gale's *Encyclopedia of Associations.*

What will you find? You can strike pay dirt or you can strike out. But even if you find nothing, there is a reward. You will develop good research skills and become reacquainted with the public library which had greatly missed your patronage.

EXAMPLES: JOBS YOU HAVE HELD

Golf Course Caddie
Evans Scholars Foundation. About 225 caddies receive renewable tuition scholarships each year. Students must be of outstanding personal character, require financial assistance, be in the top 25% of their HS class and have caddied for at least 2 years at a WGA member club. By Nov. 1. For more information, write Scholarship Committee, Western Golf Association/Evans Scholar Foundation, Golf, IL 60029.

Fast Food Worker
McDonalds and Burger King both have demonstrated serious commitments to higher education. For example, McDonald's is creating the nation's largest apprenticeship program (4,000 students in 15 states) while Burger King provides scholarships through endowments made to selected colleges and universities.

Newspaper Carrier
Thomas Ewing Education Grants for HS seniors who have been *Washington Post* carriers for at least 2 years; 33 awards ranging from $1000-$2000. Other papers have similar awards.

EXAMPLES: CLUBS

Boy Scouts
Directory of Scholarships and Loan Funds, a free booklet, lists programs open to scouts and former scouts. Send self-addressed, stamped envelope to: Learning for Life, Boy Scouts of America, 1325 Walnut Hill Lane, Irving, TX 75015.

Distributive Education Club of America (DECA)
Must be member of high school DECA chapter, have financial need and an interest in marketing or distribution. Information from chapter advisor.

4-H Clubs & Future Homemakers of America (FHA)
Scholarships for current or former 4-H members who have won state honors. Nearly 250 awards ranging from $750 to $1,500. Contact State 4-H Leader or County 4-H Agent.

EXAMPLES: ANCESTRY AND NATIONALITY

National Society Daughters of the American Revolution
Various scholarships programs for children of DAR members. Application packets from Office of the Committees, NSDAR, 1776 D Street, NW, Washington DC 20006-5392. By Feb. 15.

Descendants of Signers of Declaration of Independence
Must provide definitive proof of direct lineal descent to a signer of the Declaration of Independence to the Society's Registrar-General and become a member of the Descendants of the Signers. Applicant must also be a full-time student at a US college or university. Requests not naming an ancestor signer will not receive a reply. Annual grants total $10,000 to $11,000, averaging $1,500. Before Jan. 15. Send SASE to Mrs. Phillip Kennedy, DSDI Scholarship Committee, PO Box 224, Suncook, NH 03275..

Italian
UNICO National, 72 Burroughs Place, Bloomfield, NJ 07003. Applicant must reside in community with UNICO chapter. By April 15.

Japanese
Japanese American Citizens League, 1765 Sutter Street, San Francisco, CA 94115. Undergraduate, graduate. Performing arts, creative arts, law. For application, send SASE. Apply by March 1.

Polish
Grants Office, The Kosciuszko Foundation, 15 East 65th Street, New York, NY 10021-6595. Polish Studies, music, voice, and others. Mainly specialized, graduate and postgrad study awards. Domestic deadline Jan. 15. Exchange program deadline Nov. 15. Summer Session in Poland (March 15 deadline).

Membership Organizations
Chinese-American Foundation, Danish Brotherhood of America, Lithuanian Alliance, Polish Falcons, Daughters of Penelope, Order of AHEPA, Sons of Norway, Sons of Poland, Russian Brotherhood Organization, Many others. Addresses of all these organizations may be found in Gale's *Encyclopedia of Associations*. An increasing number may be found on the Infobahn.

EXAMPLES: DENOMINATION

Catholic

The Pro Deo and Pro Patria scholarships. Sixty two awards of $1,500 based on academic excellence. Applicant or applicant's father must be member of the Columbian Squires or Knights of Columbus. Must be used at a Catholic college. Apply by March 1. Also sponsors other scholarships, fellowships, graduate programs, student loans. Also awards for study in Canada, Mexico, Philippines, Puerto Rico. Contact Director of Scholarship Aid, Knights of Columbus, PO Box 1670, New Haven, CT 06507. Or call, 203-772-2130 x224.

Christian Scientist

Loan program. Range $2,800-$3,500 per academic year. Interest is 3% below prime. Repayment starts six months after graduation. Loans are interest-free to Christian Scientist nurses if they achieve Journal listing. The Albert Baker Fund, 5 Third St., Suite 717, San Francisco, CA 94103. By August 1.

Jewish

Up to $7,500/year for 2 years for graduate students preparing for careers in Jewish Community Center work. Write Scholarship Coordinator, JCC Association, 15 East 26th Street, New York, NY 10010. By Feb. 1.

Lutheran

Aid Association for Lutherans

Two competitive programs for AAL members only: (1) All College Scholarship Program which offers 1,000 renewable and nonrenewable awards each year, value range: $1,000-$2,500. (2) Vocational-Technical School Scholarship program, 100 renewable awards each year to graduating high school seniors. Value range is $500/year, for a maximum of 2 years. Apply by Nov. 30 to AAL, Scholarships, 4321 North Ballard Road, Appleton, WI 54919.

One college-based program: AAL members who plan to enroll at participating Lutheran school may receive a Lutheran Campus Scholarship ranging from $200 to $1,000/year. Awards made by schools. Request school list from above address.

Lutheran Brotherhood

Approximately 700 Scholarships (value to $2,000). Must be member of Lutheran Brotherhood. By Jan. 31 to Scholarship & Loan Coordinator, Lutheran Brotherhood, 625 4th Avenue South, Minneapolis, MN 55415. By January 31.

Also, approximately 500 awards (range $800 to $1,500) to Lutheran students who attend Lutheran junior and senior colleges. Selections made by schools. Awardees do not have to be members of Lutheran Brotherhood. Also a Stafford Student Loan Program Lender.

Presbyterian

Scholarships from $100 to $2,000. Undergraduate and graduate. Also grants, loans, and special minority awards. Manager, Financial Aid for Studies, Presbyterian Church in the USA, 100 Witherspoon St., Louisville, KY 40202-1396.

United Methodist

Loans and scholarships for US citizens who have been active, full members of the United Methodist Church for at least one year prior to submitting application. More information from your church or write to: Student Loans & Scholarships, The United Methodist Church, Board of Higher Education and Ministry, PO Box 871, Nashville, TN 37202.

Chapter 18
Money for Brains and Talent

The SAT has become a national industry. The money spent designing tests, administering tests, scoring tests, taking tests, teaching test skills, coaching test takers, disseminating test results, selling the names and scores of test takers to eager college recruiters, interpreting scores, analyzing scores, publicizing scores, and writing about the test, pro and con, places the SAT somewhat behind the automobile industry but far ahead of the horseradish trade as a contributor to our gross national product.

The result of all this energy resulted in the Scholastic Aptitude Test adopting a slightly new name—The Scholastic Assessment Test—and a slightly new format. The evil antonyms are gone and students have to generate answers to a few math problems on their own (as opposed to guessing via multiple choice). The initial reaction has been a nationwide panic among little Fermat wanabees (and their parents), causing test prep enrollments to double, and our GNP to soar!

Despite the prevailing attitude, this testmania still has no rational underpinnings. It is a modern addendum to the classic treatise "Popular Delusions and the Madness of Crowd." For the SAT is not an intelligence measure. It is not an aptitude measure. Despite its name change, it doesn't really assess anything. It is not a predictor of academic success. And getting high scores on it isn't always important for gaining college admission. It's only verifiable characteristics are that, one, test scores corresponds quite closely to family income. The higher the income, the higher the scores. And two, it thrives on criticism. The more it is attacked and exposed, the more it gains in universality and acceptance.

But this outburst should not turn you away. High test scores have a direct monetary application. They can cost you money or they can make money for you.

Cost you money? you ask. How? Suppose you live in a school district which emphasizes test teaching. That emphasis will raise scores. And higher scores cause property values to soar because parents from everywhere now want to move to your district so the smarts rub off on junior. Your $50,000 home with a swampy basement, shaky foundation, and a indigenous population of overweight termites is suddenly worth $100,000, a nice increase that adds $2,500 to your family contribution. Frankly, we think enterprising real estate firms should underwrite SAT preparation courses. It could be their smartest investment.

Now that we have learned how the SAT can cost you money, let's see how it can make you money. Here is what good scores can do:

1. Qualify you for a National Merit or Regent Scholarship.
2. Push you over the eligibility cutoff for collegiate academic scholarships.
3. Give you bargaining power when negotiating the content of a financial aid package. Your higher scores make you more valuable to the school because they help raise the average for the entire entering freshman class.

The hard way to raise SAT scores is to find an error in the test and appeal it. An easier way is to wait for the College Board to recenter everyone's scores (the Class of 1996 was the first to benefit from these new, higher, averages) The easiest way is to take a good SAT prep course—but take it for the practical reasons listed above and not for any mythological reasons. If a $500 investment in a SAT prep course yields a $2,000 no-need scholarship, renewed each year for four years, you have done far better with your money than the shrewdest Wall Street stockbroker.

Two national organizations are Stanley Kaplan, Ltd. (800-KAP-TEST, http://www.Kaplan.com) and The Princeton Review (800-2-REVIEW, http://www.review.com). Their "teaching" styles are very different and they have no great love for each other, but they both have great track records for raising scores. Call the above numbers for the nearest test center. You might also ask about any school-sponsored test prep courses, or local test prep services. The fees will be lower, and, usually, the results just as good. Of course, if you're really disciplined, Stanley Kaplan and The Princeton Review also publish test prep books and CD Roms for "self-study." Or you might visit Stanford Testing Program's free on-line service (WebWare for the SAT) at http://www.testprep.com.

WHERE ARE THE REWARDS FOR THE BRIGHT?
The A's & B's of Academic Scholarships (inside back cover) describes 100,000 academic awards offered at 1200 colleges; awards that range from $200 to $20,000 per year. Most of these awards, moreover, are not based on need.

DO YOU HAVE BRAINS, LEADERSHIP, TALENT?
Many scholarship opportunities are reserved for students with extraordinary abilities. There are two main ways to link up with these awards: via competitions and through recommendations of teachers, coaches, and bandmasters.

In following this route, make certain the honor you're applying for isn't going to cost you a fortune. There are many companies whose main mission is to make a profit off your achievement. They buy mailing lists of good students (e.g., those with B+ averages or better) and try to sell them everything from $50 books featuring (surprise) their very own biography and photo, to $750 trips to Washington to hobnob with the political elite.

Art and Photography
The Scholastic Art Awards. Cash, scholarships, other. Grades 7-12. The Scholastic Art & Writing Awards, 555 Broadway, New York, NY 10012.

Arts (Dance, Music, Theater, Visual Arts, Writing)
Up to $300,000 in scholarships, also, nomination to the White House Commission on Presidential Scholars and identification of talented students to colleges which may offer additional awards. HS seniors or those 17 or 18 years old by 1 Dec. the year they apply. $35 fee (may be waived in hardship cases). Nat'l Foundation for Advancement in the Arts/Arts Recognition & Talent Search, 800 Brickell Ave., #500, Miami, FL 33131. 305/377-1148, 800/970-ARTS. By 1 Nov.

Brains
1. *National Merit Scholarship Program.* Participants take the PSAT/NMSQT (in their Junior year of HS). Semifinalists are contacted by the Merit program through their HS and finalists compete for 2,000 one-time Merit Scholarships and about 4,900 other Merit Scholarships, most of which are renewable with stipend amounts that vary from $250 to $2,000+ per year for four undergraduate years. For more information, obtain *PSAT/NMSQT Student Bulletin* from your high school guidance counselor or the National Merit Scholarship Corporation, 1560 Sherman Ave., #200, Evanston, IL 60201.

2. *National Honor Society.* 250 $1,000 scholarships for members of the National Honor Society. Nominations through HS chapter. February deadline.
3. *Mensa Scholarships.* Awards to $1,000. Based on essay competition. Application from local Mensa group with SASE, by January 31.

Brains and Talent

Scholarship competition for students with outstanding academic ability (and SATs of at least 1200) or who excel in the performing or visual arts. $1,000-$5,000. No deadline. National Alliance for Education, 55 Highway 35, Suite 5, Red Bank, NJ 07701. Must pay $5 application fee. Send SASE.

Citizenship

HS seniors. Entries judged on basis of an application. (2) $1,250 awards per Soroptimist region and (1) $2,000 finalist award. Deadline December 15. Contact your local Soroptimist Club or send SASE to Soroptimist International of the Americas, Two Penn Center Plaza, #1000, Philadelphia, PA 19102.

Drama

Thespian Society. Members only scholarships through HS chapter.

Geography

The National Geography Bee is cosponsored by the National Geographic Society and Amtrak. Top prizes (to fourth- through eighth-grade participants) are three college scholarships worth $25,000, $10,000 and $5,000. (5 million contestants per year!)

General

Advisory List of National Contests, approved list of contests. $4.00 from Nat'l Assoc. of Secondary School Principals, 1904 Association Dr., Reston, VA 22091.

Leadership & Brains

1. *Century III Leaders Scholarship Program.* $142,000 in scholarships awarded annually. Program is funded by Sylvan Learning Centers and administered by Nat'l Association of Secondary School Principals. Program announcement placed in high schools in September. October deadline. Seniors only.
2. *Principal's Leadership Award (PLA).* 150 $1,000 scholarships. Applications sent to HS principal in October. December deadline. Seniors only. Program is administered by Nat'l Association of Secondary School Principals.
3. *U. S. Senate Youth Program.* 104 $2,000 scholarships to elected student government officers plus week long trip to Washington DC. Selections by state. Nominations by Nov. 15; William Randolph Hearst Foundation, 90 New Montgomery St., #1212, San Francisco, CA 94105. (800) 841-7048.
4. *Truman Scholars.* $30,000 max. over 4 years. 85 awards. You must be nominated by your college in your sophomore or junior year. Awards are for junior or senior year plus up to 3 years of grad school. Solid class standing. Outstanding potential for leadership in public service. Harry S. Truman Scholarship Foundation, 712 Jackson Place, NW, Washington, DC 20006.

Math, Engineering and Natural Sciences

Barry M. Goldwater Scholarship. Undergraduate scholarships to outstanding college sophomores and juniors who plan to pursue careers in math, engineering or the natural sciences. Tuition, fees, books, room and board, up to $7,000/year for one or two years. One scholarship to a resident of each state. Additional scholars-at-large may also be chosen (285 scholarships were awarded last year). Applicants are selected and nominated by their college. By January 15. Contact your campus faculty representative.

Math, Science and Computer Science

Tandy Technology Scholars. 100 awards of $1,000 each. Final selection based on GPA, SAT/ACT scores, excellence in math, science or computer science, and service to the community. Nominated by HS. For more information, write Tandy Technology Scholars, PO Box 298990, TCU, Fort Worth, TX 76129.

Oratory & Essays

Large awards. Lots of competition. The American Legion, Optimist International and Civitan all sponsor contests (example: about 25,000 HS students compete for a top prize of $18,000 in the American Legion's Oratorical Contest).

Poetry

The National Library of Poetry awards $24,000 per year to over 250 poets in the North American Open Poetry Contest. Send one original poem (any subject, any style, no more than 20 lines) to the National Library of Poetry, 11419 Cronridge Drive, PO Box 704, Owings Mills, MD 21117. By June 30.

Political Science

First Nationwide Network Scholarship Program. 32 awards of $1,000 each to college juniors majoring in political science, history, or government. Established to honor John F. Kennedy. Essay and application required. Call First Nationwide Network program manager at 507-931-1682 for more information.

Presidential Scholars

No application. Approximately 120 students selected from high scorers on the SAT and ACT. Also 20 students picked for achievement in the arts, as identified by the Arts Recognition & Talent Search (see above). A four-day visit to Washington. A handshake from the President. And $1,000 from the Dodge Foundation.

Science

Westinghouse Science Talent Search. HS seniors must submit a report on a research project in science, math or engineering, along with SAT/ACT scores, transcript and application. $205,000 in scholarships, ranging from $40,000 to $1,000. Deadline is late November. For applications contact Science Service, 1719 N Street, NW, Washington, DC 20036. (202) 785-2255.

Writing

1. *The Scholastic Writing Awards.* Cash, scholarships, other. Grades 7-12. Schools should have application materials. If not, write The Scholastic Art & Writing Awards, 555 Broadway, New York, NY 10012.
2. *Youth Writing Contest.* High School seniors. (1) $6,000; (1) $5,000; (1) $4,000; and (5) $1,000 scholarships. Write and submit a first person, 1200 word story about a memorable or moving experience you have had, preferably spiritual. Deadline November 28. GuidePosts, 16 E 34th St., New York, NY 10016.

Chapter 19
Money Because You Are an Athlete

A SUMMARY

Athletic scholarships are not limited to those with prowess in the big sports—football, baseball, basketball, hockey, soccer, tennis, and track. There is scholarship money for sailing, badminton, gymnastics, lacrosse, bowling, archery, fencing, rowing, synchronized swimming, skiing and volleyball.

All-star athletes don't need this book. They need an (unofficial) agent who can sort through all the offers, enticements, contracts and gifts that come their way. They might need a mechanic, too, to advise them on the relative merits of a Porsche or a Mercedes.

This chapter is for the better-than-average athlete with varsity potential in major and minor sports. What's available for this athlete? How can you link up? Here is the situation in a nutshell: There is considerable financial aid at most colleges for students who are good, but not necessarily great, athletes. This aid is either "reserved" for athletes (through designated scholarships) or awarded on a preferential basis as part of the financial aid packaging process.

The key to receiving consideration for this kind of aid lies in the student athlete's determination to market his or her talents. This marketing procedure is based on contacting the appropriate coach at the desired college and getting that coach to shepherd the student's request for admission and financial aid through the bureaucracy of the various admission and financial aid offices. All college coaches, if convinced of the student athlete's potential contribution to their team, will take an active role in facilitating the student's admission and financial requests. For example, some schools have admission representatives whose main responsibility is to coordinate referrals from the athletic department.

Here is a step-by-step outline to follow in marketing your athletic talents:

1. Start early. Discuss with your HS counselor the range of colleges for which you are academically qualified. In selecting suitable schools, keep in mind that approximately 20% of all colleges will reconsider their admission standards to "land" an athlete.
2. Talk to your HS coach about the quality of collegiate athletic programs for which you might qualify. Don't sell yourself short. Coaches need backup players as well as starters.
3. Narrow your college selection list to a manageable size, taking into consideration the quality of athletic and academic programs and your "fit" with them. In other words, you *don't* want to be a four-year bench-warmer; you *do* want to be challenged by the school's academic program (but not over- or underwhelmed).
4. Research the name of the coach in your sport at each college on your list. Best source: your high school athletic director's copy of *The National Directory of College Athletics* (there are separate editions of this book for men and women). You should probably do a follow up call to the athletic department to verify this name, and make certain that coach is still at the school and coaching your sport.

5. Draft a personal letter to each coach. This letter should include a profile of your academic interests and achievements. The letter's main part, however, should be a thorough and detailed discussion of your athletic accomplishments and be supported by statistics, clippings, letters earned, records, and honors. Include mention of any camps or clinics you've attended, and if appropriate, a videotape of yourself in action (keep it to 10 minutes, look enthusiastic, start with skills, move on to "game" highlights and make certain you're easily identifiable)! If your real value to the team is as a leader and motivator rather than a top scorer, make that clear. (Have you won any awards for sportsmanship?) Lastly, indicate you will need financial aid.

6. If your approach elicits interest from the colleges, ask the high school coach to follow up with a letter of recommendation or a phone call. You should also send the college a schedule of your games in case recruiters are nearby!

7. Now you must decide where to apply. Few coaches will take an interest in you unless your initial letter is followed by a formal application. And remember, here, as with any other application, apply as early as possible.

8. After applying, remain in touch with the college coaches. Inquire about the status of your application and request for financial aid. If possible, visit the college and sell yourself as a person and as an athlete. Get to know the coach, and make certain his or her coaching philosophy is compatible with your style!

CERTIFICATION

All students who intend to practice and play their sport at a Division I or II school during their freshman year must have their eligibility certified by a central clearinghouse. Essentially, the NCAA wants to make certain all student-athletes are exactly that, and has instituted minimum academic requirements for athletes.

Beginning in August, 1996, "qualifiers" must have a GPA of at least 2.0 in a core curriculum of 13 academic courses (a combination of English, math, social science, and natural or physical science) and have a combined SAT score (after recentering) of 820 (or an ACT score of 17). To be a Division I qualifier, you must meet slightly higher standards. The NCAA has developed a sliding scale of acceptable GPA/SAT/ACT scores. If you squeak in with an 820 SAT (or 17 ACT), you must have a 2.5 GPA to qualify. If your SATs (or ACTs) are higher than 820, you can get away with a slightly lower GPA (but never lower than a 2.0).

To register for the Clearinghouse, first read the NCAA brochure called *Making Sure You Are Eligible to Participate in College Sports*, then complete the accompanying student release form and send one copy of it (along with a check for $18) to the Clearinghouse. Give the other two copies of the form to your counselor; one to put in your HS files, the other to send to the Clearinghouse, along with a copy of your HS transcript (listing core courses). Students who qualify for a fee waiver for the SAT/ACT may also receive a fee waiver for the Clearinghouse.

Your counselors can obtain all these registration materials (which are free) by calling the Clearinghouse at (319) 337-1492. Note: Eligibility certification has no bearing on your admission to a particular Division I or II institution.

RECRUITING VIOLATIONS

The NCAA publishes a 512-page book full of rules and regulations. Violating one of these rules or regulations can quickly turn you into an "ineligible" athlete. For a brief overview of recruiting guidelines, ask your counselor for a copy of the NCAA *Guide for the College-Bound Student-Athlete*. While this 16-page pamphlet is by no means complete, it does touch on the major issues, and warn you about what kinds of behavior can cause you trouble.

When should you start worrying about these do's and don'ts? As soon as you become a "Prospective Student Athlete" (which happens when you start ninth-grade), although there's no need to become obsessive until you become a "Recruited Prospective Student Athlete." This occurs the moment a college coach (or representative of the school's "athletic interests") approaches you or a member of your family about participating in athletics at that college. "Contact" means providing you (or a member of your family) with an official visit, calling you more than once, or visiting you anywhere other than the college campus.

Commercial Scouting Services and Agents

Colleges often pay services to help them find top notch athletes. These services go around the country evaluating talent and selling this data to colleges, usually in the form of ratings booklets. Scouting services might also sell videotapes of HS games. You, however, are not likely to have any contact with these services. Why? In an effort to stem the growing perception that college sports are little more than feeders for professional teams, the NCAA keeps tightening the rules regarding recruiting and limiting the type of contact a coach may have with prospects.

As for agents, be careful. You can jeopardize your college eligibility by speaking to an unauthorized rep, by speaking to an authorized rep outside the approved contact period, or by agreeing to professional representation while still in HS or college (even if "the deal" doesn't become effective until after you finish college).

The Pros and Cons of Exposure Services

Exposure services, or placement services, represent the student in the search for athletic scholarships. These services can cost you from $500-$800 and they generally just follow the eight steps outlined previously! In other words, many people feel they're a waste of money since there is no reason why you can't "sell" yourself and save the services' fee. Also, some college coaches say they're a bit skeptical of organizations that claim they can do more for a high school student than his or her high school coach (after all, your HS coach is the person who should be most familiar with your abilities). Furthermore, you shouldn't base your choice of college on its athletic opportunities alone!

On the flip side, some exposure services are good and many students and schools are pleased with their results. From the students' perspective, it's an easy way to get their athletic profile sent to as many as 600 colleges. Students can then just sit back and wait for nibbles. From the school's perspective, since the athletes pay the fee, the school is getting perfectly good, free information on hundreds of potential student-athletes. These services are most useful for students who participate in "minor sports" (regardless of the school) or who are interested in smaller, less athletically prominent schools (regardless of the sport).

If you decide to use a placement service, make certain you choose a reputable one. Here are two suggestions: One, find a service that specializes in your sport, for example, the Collegiate Softball Connection in San Francisco; two, go with one of the biggies, College Prospects of America (http://www.jette.com/cpoa) or College Bound Student Athletes (http://www.in.net/cbsa). Both of these organizations have agents (salesmen?) scattered across the 50 states and serve thousands of students per year. Both of these organizations also recognize the need to match a student's level of athletic and academic ability with appropriate colleges and say they reject students without real athletic potential. Why? Because overselling students would cause them to lose credibility with the colleges and in a word-of-mouth type of business, you can't put a price tag on credibility.

If you have internet access, you might also look into a free service from Allsport, http://www.irc-coordinator.com.

Again, most students can do as well on their own, however, if you have questions about placement services, call the NCAA. While the NCAA doesn't make any endorsements, it can steer you clear of shady businesses. If you use a service, be careful about how it determines your fee. The NCAA prohibits them from receiving money based on the value of your scholarship.

Preferential Packaging vs. Athletic Scholarships

Preferential aid packaging can be a better deal than an athletic scholarship. If you have a personality conflict with the coach or run into a physical problem that keeps you from competing, you can lose your scholarship. The financial aid package, once it is wrapped up, will hold for a year.

Graduation Rates

Don't let headlines scare you. Most of the abuses you read about are restricted to big name (Division I) men's football and basketball programs. The fact is, most students who compete in collegiate athletic programs have a higher graduation rate than other students and fare better economically in the job market.

Locating Scholarships in Your Sport

Check your HS guidance office for a copy of Peterson's *Sports Scholarships and Athletic Programs* ($21.95). It lists colleges that offer sports scholarships (broken down by sport). Women should also get *The Women's Collegiate Sports Scholarship Guide* $3.00 from the Women's Sports Foundation, Eisenhower Park, East Meadow, NY, 11554, 1-800-227-3988.

Sports Careers

The NCAA awards more than $1 million to student-athletes (at Division I, II and III schools) who are pursuing an athletics-related career or post-graduate program. Four programs are for postgraduates; one is for undergraduates who have completed eligibility for athletically-related aid (i.e., they entered college at least five years ago). Request more information from the NCAA, 6201 College Boulevard, Overland Park, KS 66211-2422

REFERENCES FOR FURTHER READING

1. The NCAA publishes stiff rules on recruiting. Learn them! Get *The NCAA Guide for the College-Bound Student* from NCAA Publishing, address above. The brochures are sold in bundles of 50, but you may be able to buy a single copy. If not, ask your coach to order a set...they're fairly inexpensive. Another option is to read it on-line at the NCAA's Web site, http://www.ncaa.org.
2. For more comprehensive information, ask your counselor (or coach) to get a series of NCAA guides. *The NCAA Guide to Financial Aid* describes the types of financial aid available to student-athletes and the limits on individual and institutional aid. *The NCAA Guide to Recruiting* describes permissible activities for colleges to use to attract student-athletes. *The NCAA Guide to Eligibility* assists students and counselors in understanding eligibility regulations and compliance requirements. These books are updated annually, cost only $5 each and are available from the NCAA (address above).

Chapter 20
Money for Health Careers

As a budding nurse or doctor or therapist, don't limit your reading to this chapter. Or you will never blossom out into a nurse or doctor or therapist.

You'll find other money sources in different parts of this book. For instance, all the major federal student aid programs (in Chapter 10) will help pay for your medical education. Many of the states (Chapter 11) furnish help in those medical fields in which they believe they have shortages. And there is support for minority medical education. It's described in Chapter 22.

FEDERAL SUPPORT FOR THE HEALTH PROFESSIONS

Uncle Sam pours great amounts of money—almost a half billion dollars per year—into the training of health professionals. The assistance programs fall into two broad categories: Individual-based programs which fund students, and school-based programs which fund schools (which in-turn parcel out some of their money to students). To save space, we have used the following coding to denote medical fields. Check the coding before entering the table.

A—Allied Health, MA or higher
B—Chiropractic
C—Dentistry
D—Health Administration
E—Medicine
F—Nursing, Associate
G—Nursing, Diploma
H—Nursing, Baccalaureate
I—Nursing, Advanced
J—Nursing, Anesthetist
K—Nursing, Community Health
L—Nursing, Midwifery
M—Nursing, Psychiatric

N—Nutrition
O—Optometry
P—Osteopathy
Q—Pharmacy
R—Podiatry
S—Psychology, Clinical
T—Public Health, MA or higher
U—Safety, Occupational
V—Social Work
W—Therapy, Occupational
X—Therapy, Physical
Y—Therapy, Rehabilitation
Z—Veterinary Medicine

INDIVIDUAL-BASED PROGRAMS

The individual-based programs are fairly easy to locate. You apply directly to Uncle Sam or through the school you plan to attend. One bit of advice: You will gain an advantage over fellow applicants if you indicate a willingness to practice in a shortage area. Don't worry about what a shortage area is. Its definition and location will change several times between the time you apply and the time you graduate. What's important to know is that "shortage areas" are a big thing at the Department of Health & Human Services. It has "primary medical care shortage areas," "dental manpower shortage areas," "rural dental shortage areas," "vision care shortage areas," "podiatry shortage areas," "pharmacy shortage areas," "psychiatric shortage areas," even "veterinary care shortage areas."

For more information on all of Uncle's health care programs, you can visit the Department of Health and Human Services on-line at http://www.dhhs.gov. Or, you can go straight to the Bureau of Primary Health Care site at http://www.bphc.hrsa.dhhs.gov.

B-C-D-E-O-P-Q-R-S-T-Z. Health Education Assistance Loans. Medical, Dental, Osteopathic, Optometry, Podiatry, and Veterinary Medicine students may borrow $20,000 per year for total of $80,000. Other students: $12,500 per year (limit $50,000). Floating interest rate (91-day Treasury Bill average plus 3%). 6-8% insurance premium. Up to 25 years to repay. Includes Graduate students. Program is not authorized for study at foreign medical schools. Apply through school or write: HEAL, Room 8-37, 5600 Fishers Lane, Rockville, MD 20857, 301/443-1540.

C-E-O-P-Q-R-Z. Health Professions Student Loan. Tuition plus $2,500 per year. 5% interest begins to accrue 12 months after completion of training. Must show great financial need and practice in primary care. Apply through school.

E-I-K-L-P. National Health Service Corps Loan Repayment Program. The program will pay up to $25,000 each year for a minimum 2-year commitment and up to $35,000 per year for years 3 and 4. In addition, for each year served, the program will pay 39% of the participant's outstanding government and commercial education loans towards the increased Federal, State and local income taxes caused by these payments; NHSC Loan Repayment Program, Applications Section, 4350 East-West Highway, 10th fl., Bethesda, MD 20814, 800/435-6464, or National Health Service Corps, Loan Repayment Program, 2070 Chain Bridge Road, McLean, VA 22182, 800/221-9393 (in Virginia, 703/821-8955).

C-E-I-L-P. National Health Service Corps Scholarship Program. The NHSC will pay tuition, fees, books and supplies, plus a monthly stipend for up to four years. For each year of support, award recipients owe one year of full-time clinical practice in high-priority health professions shortage areas. For more information, write: NHSC, Scholarship Program, 8201 Greensboro Drive, #600, McLean, VA 22101, or call 800/638-0824 for an application packet in the fall (in VA, 703/821-8955).

C-E. Exceptional Financial Need Scholarships. All tuition plus stipend. Good for one year only. At completion of year, participants have priority for a NHSC Scholarship. Apply through school.

F-G-H-I. Nursing Student Loan Program. Up to $2,500 per year to maximum of $13,000. Need. 5% interest. Apply through school.

All Health Related Fields. Commissioned Officer Student Training & Extern Program (COSTEP) Work Program. For graduate awards, students must have completed minimum of 1 yr. graduate work in medical, dental, veterinary school. For undergraduate awards, students must have completed 2 yrs in a dietary, nursing, pharmacy, therapy, sanitary science, medical records, engineering, physician's assistant, or computer science field. For other health-related areas, students must be enrolled in master's or doctoral program. Student must return to studies following completion of the COSTEP assignment. Serve as an extern (another word for intern) in medical facilities of the Public Health Service during school breaks of 31-120 days duration. Get ensign's pay during work phases. Send for more information. COSTEP, Room 7A-07, Parklawn Bldg., 5600 Fishers Lane, Rockville, MD 20857.(800) 279-1605.

I-S-W-X-Y. Rehabilitation Training. Monthly trainee stipends. When inquiring, refer to Program 84.129. (Rehab Counseling, Physical and Occupational Therapy, Prosthetics-Orthotics, Speech Language-Pathology, Audiology, Rehab Services to the Blind and Deaf). Employment obligation or payback provisions govern rehabilitation long-term training scholarships. Department of Education, Rehabilitation Services Administration, 800 Independence Avenue, SW, Washington, DC 20202-2649.

SCHOOL-BASED PROGRAMS

School-based programs are something else. Here, the available dollars go directly to schools, and usually become part of the faculty payroll (Reason: Medical faculties are so high-priced, without federal aid to help pay their salaries, schools would have to foot the bill alone. To do this, they would have to raise tuition so high, no student could afford to enroll). Your challenge is to look for funded schools and negotiate with the Dean for some of the spoils. Or at least to take advantage of any extra student aid dollars. When writing to the addresses below, be sure to ask for a current list of funded schools—and be persistent (yet polite) in your request. The program officers with whom you deal usually won't understand why you need this information.

I-J-K-L. Several separate programs: Professional Nurse Traineeships. Advanced Nursing, Nurse Practitioners, Nurse Educators, Nurse Midwives, Nurse Anesthetist, Public Health Nurses, and other nursing specialties. Partial tuition and stipends. Contact your school for more information. Over 600 awards between all programs. Department of Health and Human Services, Division of Nursing, Room 9-36 Parklawn Bldg., 5600 Fishers Lane, Rockville, MD 20857.

D-T. (1) Traineeships in Graduate Programs of Health Administration; (2) Graduate Level Public Health Traineeships. Annual stipends and/or tuition assistance, awarded by the educational institution receiving a grant. Division of Associated and Dental Health Professions, HRSA, 5600 Fishers Lane, Rm. 8C-09, Rockville, MD 20857.

M-S-V. Mental Health Research (biomedical and behavioral). National Research Service awards for individual fellows. Funded through participating schools. Pre-doctoral stipend, $10,000. Post-doctoral stipend, $19,000 to #32,300 depending on years of experience. Grants Management Branch—National Institute of Mental Health, 5600 Fishers Lane, Rm. 7C-15, Rockville, MD 20857.

V. Child Welfare Training Grants. Social work or child welfare training programs. Awarded by school. Write for school list. Children's Bureau, 370 L'Enfant Promenade SW, Washington, DC 20447.

U. Occupational Safety & Health Training Grants. Paraprofessional, undergraduate and graduate level. Refer to Program 13.263 (mostly graduate level). Public Health Service, 5600 Fishers Lane, Rockville, MD 20857.

MILITARY MEDICAL AND NURSING PROGRAMS

Armed Forces Health Professions Financial Assistance Program

Specialized (residency) training for graduate physicians. Annual $15,000 grant plus generous monthly stipend and educational expenses. Service obligation. Each branch of the service has its own point of contact. Write for fact sheets:

Army	Navy	Air Force
HQ, DA (SGPS-PDO)	Medical Command, US Navy	Dir. of Health Professionals
5109 Leesburg Pike, #638	BUMED-512	HQ, USAF Recruiting Service
Falls Church, VA 22041	Washington, DC 20372-5120	Randolph AFB, TX 76150
703-756-8114	202-653-1318	800-531-5980

F. Edward Hebert School of Medicine

Armed Forces Health Professions Scholarship Program. Medicine, osteopathy, optometry, clinical psychology (Ph.D.), veterinary and nurse anesthesia (Master's degree). Monthly stipend plus tuition, fees and books, lab expenses, educational services. Minimum seven year service obligation. 165 students each year. Request scholarship fact sheet from the Asst. Secretary of Defense for Health Affairs, The Pentagon, Washington, DC 20301-1200. For catalogue, write F. Edward Hebert School of Medicine, Admissions Office, 4301 Jones Bridge Rd., Bethesda, MD 20814; 800-772-1743.

ROTC Nurse Program (Army, Navy, Air Force)

Students at an approved nursing school affiliated with an Army, Navy, or Air Force ROTC unit. 2, 3, 4 year scholarships; tuition, textbooks, and fees, plus a monthly stipend (for example, $180/month in the Air Force; $150/month in the Navy). Service obligation.

Army	Navy	Air Force
Army ROTC	Commander	HQ AFROTC
Attn: ATCC-N	Navy Recruiting Command	Scholarship Actions Section
Ft. Monroe, VA 23651	(Code 314)	551 East Maxwell Blvd.
800-USA-ROTC	801 N. Randolph Street.	Maxwell AFB, AL 36112
	Arlington, VA 22203	
	800-USA-NAVY	

AF ROTC Pre-Health Professions Program

Pre-medicine. Attend a school offering AF ROTC. 2 and 3 year scholarships. Tuition, textbooks, fees, plus $180/month. Service obligation. HQ AFROTC Recruiting Division, 551 East Maxwell Blvd, Maxwell AFB, AL 36112-6106.

PRIVATE PROGRAMS

Dental Assistant

Student Scholarship. $100/$1,000. By Sept. 1. Juliette A. Southard Scholarship Trust Fund, American Dental Assistants Association, 203 North LaSalle Street, #1320, Chicago, IL 60601.

Dental Hygienist

Numerous AA, BA, MA, Ph.D. awards to enrolled dental hygiene students. To $1,500. Also, 25 $1,000 scholarships sponsored by Proctor and Gamble. ADHA Institute for Oral Health, 444 N. Michigan, #3400, Chicago, IL 60611. By May 1.

Dental Lab Technology

Up to 25 scholarships per year. Maximum annual award for dental students is $2,500. Apply by June 15. Maximum annual award for allied dental health students is $1,000. Apply by August 15. ADA Endowment and Assistance Fund, 211 E. Chicago Ave., Suite 820, Chicago, IL 60611.

Medicine

Research Training Fellowships consist of a $14,500 stipend plus a $5,000 research allowance and a $5,000 institutional allowance. These fellowships enable sixty medical students to do full-time research for one year (renewable for an additional year). Additional grant programs as well. For more information and a fact sheet, write Howard Hughes Medical Institute, 4000 Jones Bridge Road, Chevy Chase, MD 20815-6789, or http://www.hhmi.org.

Medicine

Loans to help you out during your residency. Up to $8,000. Interest rate equals the 91-day T-bill plus 2.5% increasing to the 91-day T-bill plus 2.75% during repayment. For more information, call The Access Group at 1-800-282-1550.

Medicine, Nursing and Therapy (Occupational and Physical)

Medicine, Nursing, Occupational and Physical Therapy scholarships for students sponsored by their local DAR chapters. A variety of programs with amounts ranging from $500 to $4,000. Applications from DAR Scholarship Committee, 1776 D Street, NW, Washington, DC 20006-5392. Various deadlines. Ask for complete listing of awards.

Medical and Biological Sciences

Scholarships and Fellowships. Howard Hughes Medical Institute. College seniors or first-year graduate students. Study leading to doctoral degrees in biological/medical sciences. 80 awards per year, consisting of $14,500 stipend plus $14,000 cost-of-education allowance to the fellowship institution. Renewable for up to five years. Office of Grants and Special Programs, Howard Hughes Medical Institute, 4000 Jones Bridge Road, Chevy Chase MD 20815. http://www.hhmi.org.

Nursing

Information on scholarships, loans, grants, fellowships, awards. Send $16.95 (postpaid) for the book *Scholarships and Loans for Nursing Education 1995/96*, Publication No. 41-2683; prepayment must accompany order. National League for Nursing, 350 Hudson St., New York, NY 10014.

Nursing (Advanced)

Scholarship for registered nurses, members of a national, professional nursing association, for advanced degrees. Masters and doctoral. $2,500-$10,000. Full-time student at master's level, full-time or part-time at doctoral level. Send $5 for kit by Feb. 1. Nurses' Educational Funds, Inc., 555 W. 57th St., 13th Floor, New York, NY 10019.

Physician Assistant

For a brochure listing financial assistance sources, write American Academy of Physician Assistants, 950 North Washington Street, Alexandria, VA 22314-1552.

Surgical Technology

One $500 award and several $250 awards. For students currently enrolled in CAAHEP-accredited surgical technology programs. Association of Surgical Technologists, 7108-C S. Alton Way, #100, Englewood, CO 80112. By March 1.

Therapy (Physical, Occupational, Music, Hearing Audiology, Speech Language Pathology and Recreational Therapy)

500 awards per year, $500-$1,500 junior/senior undergraduate and graduate scholarships. National AMBUCS Scholarships for Therapists, P.O. Box 5127, High Point, NC 27262. 912/888-6052. Deadline is April 15.

Therapy (Respiratory)

Various scholarships and awards, $500-$2,500. American Respiratory Care Foundation, 11030 Ables Lane, Dallas, TX 75229. By June 30

Chapter 21
Money for Other Career Interests

The best way to capitalize on your career interest is through cooperative education (Chapter 12). The next best way is to enroll in a school with a strong reputation in your career field (e.g., Agriculture—*Iowa State*; Hotel Management—*Cornell*). Strong departments usually attract scholarship funds. These funds, however, do not start flowing until you declare your major. The third—and hardest method—is to look for portable scholarships that will fund your major at any accredited school. The list that follows is illustrative, rather than complete. To dig for additional awards, contact the organizations that provide career information in your field of interest (you'll find them in *Need a Lift?*) and the professional associations which serve these careers (locate these using a search engine on the World Wide Web or Gale's *Encyclopedia of Associations*). **When writing, always enclose a self-addressed, stamped business-size envelope (SASE).**

Accounting
1. National Society of Public Accountants. 22 $500-1,000 awards; 1 $2,000 award. Undergraduates only. B+ GPA. By Mar. 10. Must be a US or Canadian citizen attending an accredited US school. Nat'l Society of Public Accountants Scholarship Foundation, 1010 N. Fairfax St., Alexandria, VA 22314.
2. Robert Kaufman Memorial Scholarships. Up to 20 awards, from $250 to $5000. Undergrads who plan to pursue accounting can get more information from the Independent Accountants International Education Fund, 9200 S. Dadeland Blvd., Suite 510, Miami, FL 33156. By 1 March.

Architecture
American Institute of Architects offers undergrad and graduate scholarships. Undergrad Awards: Applications through an accredited school or its scholarship committee. From $500-$2,500. By Feb. 1. Graduate and professional awards from $1,000-$2,500. No later than Feb. 15th. Applications from AIA, Scholarship Programs, 1735 New York Ave., NW, Washington, DC 20006, http://www.aia.org.

Art & Architecture
Cooper Union (New York City). Extremely competitive admissions. All admitted students receive a full scholarship for the duration of their study.

Education
45 at $1,000, one at $2,000, and one at $500. International grants to HS seniors planning on a teaching career. Scholarship Grants, Phi Delta Kappa, PO Box 789, Bloomington, IN 47402. Request application in October, due by January 31.

Engineering (Civil/Construction)
40-60 renewable undergrad awards of $1,500/yr. 2-4 graduate awards of up to $7,500. Director of Programs, AGC Education & Research Foundation, 1957 E St., NW, Washington, DC 20006. By November 1. (202) 393-2040.

Engineering (Materials)
34 $500 scholarships, 3 $2,000 scholarships. Undergraduate students majoring

in materials science and engineering (metallurgy, ceramics, ceramics engineering, polymers, polymer engineering, composites, composite engineering). Citizen of US, Canada, or Mexico. ASM, Materials Park, OH 44073. By June 15.

Engineering (Mining)
100+ scholarships up to $2,000. From the Society for Mining, Metallurgy, and Exploration. Inquire through your college.

Engineering
Nat'l Society of Professional Engineers. Award was suspended for 1995/96. If reactivated, applicants must be in top 25% of HS class. US citizen. 3.0 GPA. V-500, M-600. 90 scholarships from $1,000 to $4,000. Financial need; interview. Renewable. Some reserved for minorities, women, and graduate students. NSPE Education Foundation, 1420 King St., Alexandria, VA 22314. By Dec. 1.

Engineering
400 full tuition scholarships at participating colleges for students pursuing careers in engineering. For more information and a list of schools, write General Motors, Placement and College Relations, 3044 West Grand, Detroit, MI 48202.

Enology & Viticulture
Several awards to graduate students and undergrads (enrolled in a 4-year degree program) majoring in enology or other science basic to the wine and grape industry. Applicants must meet minimum GPA requirements. By March 1. American Society for Enology and Viticulture, PO Box 1855, Davis, CA 95617.

Entomology
Several undergrad scholarships annually. $1,500. Major in biology, entomology, zoology, or related science at recognized school in U. S., Canada, Mexico. Min. of 30 semester hrs. accumulated. Send SASE to Undergraduate Scholarship Application, ESA, 9301 Annapolis Road, Lanham, MD 20706. By May 31.

Family and Consumer Science
National and International fellowships. $3,000-$5,000. For more information, write AAFCS, 1555 King St., Alexandria, VA 22314.

Food (Management, Dietetics, Culinary Arts, etc.)
100+ undergrad scholarships. 3.0 GPA. $1,000-$10,000. Diane Woodworth, Scholarship Services, The Educational Foundation of the National Restaurant Assoc., 250 South Wacker Drive, Suite 1400, Chicago, IL 60606, http://www.restaurant.org, (312) 715-1010. By March 1.

Food (Management)
Local branches offer $100 to $500 grants totalling $90,000/ year. Internat'l Food Service Executives, 1100 S. State Road 7, #103, Margate, FL 33068. By Feb 1.

Food (Science and Technology)
118 undergrad and grad scholarships. $750-$5,000. Scholarship Dept., Institute of Food Technologists, 221 N. LaSalle St., #300, Chicago, IL 60601. By Feb. 1 for juniors, seniors and graduate students, Feb. 15 for freshmen, and March 1 for sophomores.

Foreign Study
The Rotary Foundation offers three types of awards: Academic-Year Ambassadorial Scholarships of up to $22,000 for one year of study in another country

(undergrad, graduate or vocational study), Multi-Year Ambassadorial Scholarships of up to $11,000 per year for two or three years, and Cultural Ambassadorial Scholarships for intensive language study (3 to 6 months). Apply through local Rotary Club. For an application, contact your local club or write: The Rotary Foundation, One Rotary Center, 1560 Sherman Ave., Evanston, IL, 60201. Deadlines determined by individual clubs, and may be as early as March..

Geology

About 250 grants of up to $2,000. Masters/doctoral thesis research at universities in U.S., Canada, Mexico, Central America. Members and nonmembers eligible. Contact Research Grants Administrator, Geological Soc. of America, PO Box 9140, Boulder, CO 80301, http://www.geosociety.org. By Feb. 15.

Geophysics

Need and competence. 60-100 awards. Average: $1,200. Students taking course work directed toward career in Geophysics. Scholarship Committee, SEG Foundation, PO Box 702740, Tulsa, OK 74170. By March 1.

Graphic Arts

Over 300 scholarships from $500-$1,500. Renewable. National Scholarship Trust Fund, 4615 Forbes Ave., Pittsburgh, PA 15213. By Mar. 15. (Some graduate awards as well, ranging from $500 to $4,000. By Jan. 10.)

History

Daughters of the American Revolution. $2,000/year. Renewable. HS senior. Top third of class. Major in American History. All students are judged on the basis of academic excellence, commitment to the field of study and financial need. All applications must be sponsored by the local DAR Chapter. Send applications to the DAR Scholarship Committee State Chair by 1 Feb. One winner from each state is submitted to the National Chair. For more information, send SASE to: NSDAR, Office of the Committees, Scholarships, 1776 D St., NW, Washington, DC 20006.

Horticulture

1. *Bedding Plants Foundation.* $500-$2,000 undergrad and $1,000-$2,000 graduate scholarships. Renewable. By April 1. Bedding Plants Foundation, PO Box 27241, Lansing, MI 48909. (517) 694-8537.
2. *American Orchid Society.* Grants for experimental projects and research on orchids in areas such as biological research, conservation, ecology. $500-$12,000. Up to 3 years working on orchid-related dissertation projects that lead to the Ph.D. Must be enrolled full-time in a doctoral program of an accredited academic institution. Application by Jan. 1 or Aug. 1. American Orchid Society, 6000 South Olive Ave., West Palm Beach, FL 33405.

International Education

1. *Foreign Language and Area Studies* (FLAS) program to stimulate foreign language fluency and develop a pool of international experts. About 600 academic year awards ($8,000 each) and 350 summer fellowships ($1,500 each). Students apply through funded institutions. For more information and a school list write: Center for International Education, FLAS Fellowships, US Department of Education, Washington, DC 20202-5331.
2. *National Security Education Program.* Federal scholarships for foreign languages and international affairs. Nearly 500 scholarships for undergrads (800-618-673-NESP) and graduate students (800-498-9360).

Journalism

Excellent booklet listing several million in print journalism scholarships. Write for *The Journalist's Road to Success: A Career and Scholarship Guide*. 150 pages. Has minority section. Dow Jones Newspaper Fund, Inc., PO Box 300, Princeton, NJ 08543-0300. $3.00/copy prepaid. 800-DOW-FUND

Librarianship

List of scholarships available for Library Technical Assistants and Librarians. Ask for booklet *Financial Assistance for Library and Information Studies*, include $1.00. Standing Committee on Education, American Library Association, 50 E. Huron St., Chicago, IL 60611, http://www.ala.org.

Merchant Marine

$750/quarter subsistence allowance for students at CA, ME, MA, NY, TX, and Great Lakes Maritime Academies. Service obligation. Academies Program Officer, Maritime Administration, 400 Seventh St., SW, Washington, DC 20590.

Music

Request Scholarship and Awards Chart, listing hundreds of opportunities. Include $1.00 for the chart and postage. Mail to: National Federation of Music Clubs Headquarters, 1336 N. Delaware St., Indianapolis, IN 46202.

Naval Architecture

Ship design. All tuition paid. Top students. High SAT. Webb Institute, Crescent Beach Rd., Glen Cove, NY 11542-1398.

Private Club Management

Scholarships. Apply after first year of college. Essay, 2.5 GPA required. The Club Foundation, 1733 King St., Alexandria, VA 22314. By June 1.

Public Service

$500 and $1,000 awards. Careers in Public Service. Public Employees Roundtable scholarships. Undergrad and graduate level. 3.5 GPA. Must plan to pursue career in Public Service. Send SASE to PER, PO Box 14270, Washington, DC 20044-4270, or (202) 927-5000. Applications due by April 15.

Real Estate Appraisers

50 scholarships. $3,000 for grad. students, $2,000 for undergrads. Appraisal Inst. Education Trust, 875 N. Michigan, #2400. Chicago, IL 60611. By Mar. 15.

Science and Engineering

Bell & Howell Scholarships. Electronics, engineering technology, computer science, business. Scores, transcript. 60 $11,000 scholarships ($2,750/yr. for 4 years). Bell & Howell Education Group, Inc., B & H Science & Engineering Scholarship, 1 Tower Lane. Suite 1000, Villa Park, IL 60181.

Special Education

Special Education Career preparation. Program funded through schools. For school list, write: Division of Personnel Preparation, Special Education Programs, Department of Education, Washington, DC 20202.

Travel Agents

American Society of Travel Agents Scholarship Fund. Undergrad and graduate level, 2.5 GPA, 24 scholarships, $500-3,000. ASTA Scholarship Foundation, 1101 King St., Alexandria, VA 22314. By July 26.

Chapter 22
Money for Minorities and Women

Many of you have a head start, an edge, in the competition for need-based aid. Why? Because, statistically, the income of minority families is lower than that of their majority peers, and because women earn less than men who hold equal positions. Furthermore, as part of their effort to retain more students, schools are likely to give minorities and women more favorable aid packages (e.g., more grants than loans). The General Accounting Office (GAO) has shown that grant money has a strong effect on low-income student persistence; that an additional $1,000 in grant funds means a 14% decrease in dropout rates while a $1,000 increase in loan aid means a 3% increase in dropout rates. (The GAO defines low income as income below $21,000.) What these numbers say is that for once you have a leg up. You are a stride ahead. Take advantage of that lead and only after you have gone the traditional, need-based route, navigated it with savvy and control, should you look for the icing, found in this chapter.

In addition to the resources described in this chapter, you should also request the 1994 edition of *Higher Education Opportunities for Minorities and Women* from the US Department of Education, Higher Education Programs, 400 Maryland Avenue, SW, Portals C-80, Washington DC 20202.

FEDERAL ASSISTANCE TO MINORITIES

All Minorities

Graduate Fellowship Program. Graduate study in science, mathematics, engineering. Master's level and doctorate. Up to three years of support. Approximately $14,400 per year. By early Nov. Write: NSF Graduate Research Fellowship Program, Oak Ridge Associated Universities, PO Box 3010, Oak Ridge, TN 37831. By early September.

Minority Access to Research Careers. Biomedical science. Funded through schools with substantial minority student bodies. Undergraduate through graduate level. For school list, write to MARC Program, National Institute of General Medical Sciences, National Institutes of Health, Westwood Bldg., rm. 950, Bethesda, MD 20892.

Minority Participation in Graduate Education Programs. $6 million program to encourage minority students to pursue graduate education. Funded through 73 colleges. For school list: Office of Higher Education Program Services, Dept. of Education, 400 Maryland Ave., SW, Washington DC, 20202

Native Americans

Native American Fellowship Program. Need-based program for eligible Indian students in undergrad programs in business, engineering, natural resources, Graduate programs in education, law, medicine, psychology, natural resources, business, engineering, clinical psychology. All tuition and stipends. Apply through your tribe or area office of Indian Education Programs. If you do not know this information, or to request a list of additional resources, call the Postsecondary Education Branch of the Bureau of Indian Affairs at 202/ 208-4871. By Jan. 1.

Indian Health Service Scholarships. Allied health fields to include pharmacy and nursing. Two programs: 1. Preparatory Scholarship Program. Two years. 2. Health Professions Scholarship Program. Both restricted to American Indians and Alaskan natives. Tuition plus stipend. Also, a loan repayment program and extern (student) employment program. Apply to Indian Health Service, Twinbrook Plaza, Suite 100, 12300 Twinbrook Parkway, Rockville, MD 20857. By May 1.

Native American Scholarship Fund. Two programs. MESBEC (math, engineering, science, business, education, computers) is for high-potential Native American students in any of these fields. The NALE (Native American Leadership in Education) program is for Native American paraprofessionals who are working in education now to return to college and earn education degrees and/or credentials. Students in both programs should have high GPAs and test scores. Contact Lynette Charlie, Director of Recruiting, 8200 Mountain Road NE #203, Albuquerque, NM 87110. (505) 262-2351.

PRIVATE ASSISTANCE FOR MINORITIES

All Minorities

Accounting. Undergrad and graduate for enrolled students. Approximately 400 merit and need-based awards. Individual grants up to $5,000. Apply by July 1. Manager, Minority Recruitment, American Institute of Certified Public Accountants, 1211 Avenue of the Americas, New York, By 10036-8775.

Architecture. 20 awards, $500-$2,500. Renewable. Nomination by HS counselor, school, professional architect. Nomination deadline is Dec 1. Open to HS seniors and college freshmen. Nomination forms from AIA, Scholarship Program, 1735 New York Avenue, NW, Washington, DC 20006.

Dental Hygienists. For at least the second year of dental hygiene curriculum. To $1,500. Also $1,000 for student accepted into entry level dental hygiene program in certain areas. American Dental Hygienists Assoc., Institute for Oral Health, Suite 3400, 444 N. Michigan, Chicago, IL 60611. By May 1.

Dentistry. 20-30 Scholarships of $1,000 for first year in dental school. By May 1 to American Fund for Dental Health, 211 East Chicago Ave., #820, Chicago, IL 60611.

Engineering. $2 million plus awarded through schools. Schools select. Obtain scholarship guide and list of funded schools from National Action Council of Minorities in Engineering, 3 West 35th Street, New York, 10001-2281.

Engineering. Tuition, fees, stipend of $6,000/year. US citizen. Must carry full academic load towards a master's degree in engineering and intern for a member employer during summer. Also, $12,000 stipends for students enrolled in Ph.D. programs. National Consortium for Graduate Degrees for Minorities in Engineering and Science, Inc., Executive Director, GEM Fellowships, Box 537, Notre Dame, IN 46556. 219-631-7771. By Dec. 1.

General Studies. Minority members of the United Methodist Church (for at least 1 year prior) Ethnic Scholarships, value: $100 to $1,000. Contact your church for more information.

General Studies. Minority Leadership Program, $2,000 and $5,000 awards. Washington Center for Internships and Academic Semesters, 1101 14th Street NW, #500, Washington, DC 20005

General Studies. 1. Student Opportunity Scholarships for Communicant members of the Presbyterian Church, $100-$1,400. By April 1. 2. Native American Education Grant Program for Indians, Aleuts, and Eskimos pursuing post-secondary education. $200-$1,500. By June 1. Other scholarships, grants, loans. Manager, Financial Aid for Studies, Presbyterian Church, 100 Witherspoon St., Louisville, KY 40202-1396.

Geosciences. 80+ scholarships. Undergrad/grad. Undergrad up to $10,000/yr. Graduate to $4,000/yr. AGI-MPP, American Geological Institute, 4220 King St., Alexandria, VA 22302-1507. By Feb. 1.

Humanities. Tuition plus $10,500 stipend. Up to four years support leading to Ph.D. CIC Pre-doctoral Fellowships Program in Humanities, Kirkwood Hall 111, Indiana University, Bloomington, IN 47405. U. S. Citizen. By Jan.1.

Legal Training for the Disadvantaged. Last year, this $3 million program prepared students for entry into law school with $7,000 stipend for 1st year, $5,000 for 2nd and 3rd years. Also six week summer institutes and help with law school placement. The program has been zeroed out of the current federal budget, but may be re-instated. Write Council on Legal Education Opportunity, 1420 N Street., NW, Terrace One, Washington, DC 20005. Apply between Sept. 1 and Feb. 1.

Sciences. CIC Pre-doctoral Fellowships Program in the Sciences, Kirkwood Hall 111, Indiana University, Bloomington, IN 47405. By Jan.1. Will be funded through eligible institution.

Social Sciences. Tuition plus $10,000 stipend. Up to five years support leading to Ph.D. CIC Pre-doctoral Fellowships Program, Kirkwood 111, Indiana University, Bloomington, IN 47405. U.S. Citizen. By Jan.1.

African American

General Studies. National Achievement Scholarship Program for Outstanding Negro Students. African-American students enter the competition when they take the PSAT/NMSQT (in their junior year of HS). Finalists compete for 400 nonrenewable $2,000 scholarships, and about 400 other awards, most of which are renewable (and worth $250-$2,000 per year). For more information, obtain the PSAT/NMSQT Student Bulletin from your HS counselor or write the National Merit Scholarship Corp., 1560 Sherman Avenue, Suite 200, Evanston, IL 60201.

Law. Accepted by law school, also awards for public interest law. Preferred consideration for need and under 35 years of age. Earl Warren Legal Training Program, 99 Hudson St., Suite 1600, New York, By 10013. By April 1.

Latino

Communications. Scholarships to exceptional Latino students who are pursuing a degree in journalism, communications, or media and who have a commitment upon graduation to pursue a career in these fields, including communications, or entertainment law. Applicants must meet financial and academic criteria. Write: MALDEF, 634 S. Spring St., 11th Floor, Los Angeles, CA 90014. By June 30.

Engineering. General Motors/LULAC Scholarship. Thirty $2,000 scholarships to engineering majors with at least a 3.25 GPA. Send SASE to LULAC National Educational Service Centers, 2100 M Street NW, #602, Washington, DC 20037. By August 1. General Electric sponsors engineering awards as well (via LULAC).

General Studies. LULAC National Scholarship Fund. Students must request scholarship applications from the LULAC council in their community. For list of participating councils, send a SASE to LULAC National Educational Service Centers, 2100 M Street NW, #602, Washington, DC 20037. Currently enrolled students only.

General Studies. Awards to enrolled undergraduate and graduate students with at least fifteen credit hours. SASE to National Hispanic Scholarship Fund, ATTN: Selection Committee, PO Box 728, Novato, CA 94948. Between August 15 and October 1.

General Studies. National Hispanic Recognition Program identifies academically outstanding Hispanic students and furnishes their names to colleges and universities to encourage recruitment and financial support. To be eligible, students must take the PSAT/NMSQT in the fall of their Junior year, identify themselves as being of Hispanic descent, and indicate that they'd like to participate in the program. No monetary awards, but may lead to collegiate awards. Ask your HS counselor for more information, or write: The College Board, National Hispanic Scholar Recognition Program, 1717 Massachusetts Ave., NW, Suite 401, Washington, DC 20036.

Law. Scholarships to outstanding Latino law students who have demonstrated commitment to serve the Latino community upon graduation. Applicants must meet financial and academic criteria. Write: MALDEF, 634 S. Spring St., 11th Floor, Los Angeles, CA 90014. By June 30.

Native American

Graduate Study. Over 400 awards/year (although, currently, they're having a funding shortage). Master's, doctorate and professional level assistance to needy students who are at least 1/4 American Indian or enrolled members of federally-recognized tribes. Write: American Indian Graduate Center, 4520 Montgomery Blvd., NE, #1-B, Albuquerque, NM 87109. 505/881-4584. By May 1. $10 application fee.

PRIVATE AID TO WOMEN

A tip to returning women: If you have small children who require care while you attend class, be sure to let the college know. Your student expense budget should be raised to reflect child care expenses. The larger expense budget increases your need and will help you qualify for more aid.

Aerospace Science or Engineering

Amelia Earhart Fellowship Awards, $6,000 grants for graduate students. Women only. Zonta International Foundation, 557 W. Randolph St., Chicago, IL 60661. By Nov. 1.

Athletics

Complete listing of colleges and universities offering athletic scholarships. Guide is available for $3.00 from Women's Sports Foundation, Eisenhower Park, East Meadow, New York, 11554.

Engineering

1. Society of Women Engineers. Approximately 80 scholarships, value from $1,000 to $5,000. Society of Women Engineers, 120 Wall Street, 11th floor, New York, NY 10005.

2. Bell Labs Engineering. 15 Scholarships. All college costs. Recommendations from counselor, teachers, principal. AT&T Bell Laboratories, ATTN: ESP Admin., 101 Crawfords Corner Road, Box 1030, Holmdel, NJ 07733. Jan. 15 deadline. Also, summer programs.

3. BPW Loan Fund for Women in Engineering Studies. $5,000 per year, 7% interest. By April 15. For further information, send SASE with 2 first class stamps to BPW Foundation, 2012 Massachusetts Avenue, NW, Washington, DC 20036.

General

$5 million annually in local, state, and national awards. Apply early in junior year of high school. Contestants are evaluated in areas of scholastic achievement (20%), fitness (15%), presence and composure (15%), creative and performing arts (25%), and judges interviews (25%). America's Junior Miss, Dept. DMO, PO Box 2786, Mobile, AL 36652. Awards count as taxable income.

General

Fellowships and grants for advanced research, graduate study, and community service. Women, US citizen. Application by Nov. 15 for dissertation/postdoc. By Feb. 1 for research and project grants. American Association of University Women, Educational Foundation Fellowships and Grants, PO Box 4030, Iowa City, IA 52243-4030, (319) 337-1716.

General

Kappa Kappa Gamma awards are available only to members of Kappa Kappa Gamma. For complete information, send SASE (with 55 cents) to KKG Foundation, PO Box 38, Columbus, OH 43216-0038. Please note your chapter membership on your request. Also, graduate students should state whether they are studying full- or part-time. Application deadline, February 1.

Golf

1. Gloria Fecht Memorial Scholarship Fund. 15-20 $1,000-$3,000 per year academic scholarships for qualified student golfers who are California residents and either from Southern California or attending Southern California schools. No specific level of golfing skill required. Applications due March 1. Gloria Fecht Memorial Scholarship Fund, 402 W. Arrow Hwy., Suite 10, San Dimas, CA 91773.

2. Women's Western Golf Foundation. Undergraduate scholarships. $8,000 ($2,000/yr.) toward room, board, tuition, fees. Interest in golf is important; golfing ability is not. Selected on basis of academic achievement, financial need, excellence of character. Contact Mrs. Richard Willis, 393 Ramsay Road, Deerfield, IL 60015. Request preliminary application by March 1, return by March 15.

Older Women

Four programs, each with its own eligibility requirements. $500 to $2,000. BPW Career Advancement, Avon Foundation Scholarship for Women in Business Studies, New York Life Scholarship for Women in the Health Professions. Wyeth-Ayerst Scholarship for Women in Graduate Medical and Health Business Programs. Apply by April 15. For further information and application forms, send SASE with 2 first class stamps after Oct. 1 to Scholarships, BPW Foundation, 2012 Massachusetts Avenue, NW, Washington, DC 20036, 202/296-9118.

Chapter 23
Special Situations: Non-Traditional Students

PHYSICALLY DISABLED

Physically disabled students frequently incur special expenses while attending college. Make sure these expenses are reflected in your student budget (see Chapter 6). This, in turn, will increase your need and you'll qualify for more aid.

Your best source of information on special student aid is the Office of Vocational Rehabilitation in your state's education department.

For additional information, write: HEATH Resource Center, One Dupont Circle, NW, Suite 800, Washington, DC 20036-1193. 800-544-3284 or (202) 939-9320. You may also learn more about HEATH through the American Council on Education web site, http://www.acenet.edu. HEATH is the national clearinghouse on post-secondary education for individuals with disabilities, so be specific about your situation to make certain you receive the correct materials. As a start, request their publications entitled *Financial Aid for Students with Disabilities* and *Make the Most of Your Opportunities.*

Another large clearinghouse is the National Information Center for Children and Youth with Disabilities. Copies of their publications are available on their Web site, http://aed.org/nichcy/index.html, or you can contact them at PO Box 1492, Washington DC, 20013, 800/695-0285. Again, the more specific you are with your requests, the more helpful the information you receive will be.

Finally, check your library for the most recent edition of *Financial Aid for the Disabled and Their Families,* Reference Service Press, 1100 Industrial Road, #9, San Carlos, CA 94070. The book costs around $40 and lists about 900 aid sources available to people with disabilities, including a list of state sources of benefits.

Here are some national programs that provide good work and some assistance:

The Alexander Graham Bell Association for the Deaf, 3417 Volta Place, NW, Washington, DC 20007, sponsors an annual scholarship awards program for auditory-oral profoundly or severely deaf college students. $250 to $1,000. Request application ASAP and submit by April 1.

American Council of the Blind offers 24 scholarships ($500 to $4,000). By March 1. Contact Scholarship Administrator, ACB, 1155 15th St. NW, Suite 720, Washington, DC 20005. 202-467-5081.

National Association of the Deaf. William C. Stokoe Scholarship. For deaf students pursuing part-or full-time graduate studies in field related to Sign Language or the Deaf Community. $1,000. Contact Stokoe Scholarship Secretary, National Assoc. of the Deaf, 814 Thayer Avenue, Silver Spring, MD 20910. By March 15.

Recording for the Blind and Dyslexic. Learning Through Listening Awards to HS seniors with specific learning disabilities who plan to continue their education. Three awards, $6,000 each. By Feb. 1. Public Affairs Dept., Recording for the Blind and Dyslexic, 20 Roszel Rd., Princeton, NJ 08540.

Sertoma International. Scholarship Program for students with hearing loss pursuing four-year college degrees. Ten awards, $1,000 each. Applicants must have documented hearing loss and be a full-time entering or continuing student. By May 1. SASE to Optical/Phonic Ear Scholarships, Sertoma (SERvice to MANkind), 1912 East Meyer Blvd., Kansas City, MO 64132.

PART-TIMERS

Most financial aid is based on being at least a half-time student. But take heart. Uncle's definition of "half-time" is more generous than at most schools, therefore, we urge you to apply for federal student aid even if you aren't sure what your status will be (see Chapter 10). Also, under current law, colleges must set aside some of their SEOG and Federal Work-study fund for assistance to less than half-time (i.e., part-time) students. Several states also help part-timers, so check with them as well (addresses in Chapter 11).

Our Suggestion: Take another course, and boost your status to half-time.

ARE YOU 50, 60 OR OLDER?

If you plan to study at least half-time, most financial aid is awarded on the basis of need and not age. Hence, you can freely compete with those who are just out of high school and anybody else for all available financial aid.

If you plan to take just a few courses, many schools will offer you reduced tuition. Many will even let you attend courses for free or on a space available basis.

Similarly, many states also reduce tuition for older citizens, for example, Alabama, Arkansas, Colorado, Connecticut, Delaware, Guam, Illinois, Iowa, Kentucky, Louisiana, Maine, Minnesota, Mississippi, Montana, Nebraska, New Hampshire, New Mexico, North Carolina, Rhode Island, South Carolina, Tennessee, Texas, Vermont, Virginia, Washington, Wisconsin, and Wyoming. Some states waive tuition entirely. Eligibility varies from state to state, but generally, students must be state residents age 60+ and attend state schools. Sometimes the discount is given to students only on a space available basis. Check your local college or state higher education agency (addresses in Chapter 11).

Other sources of college information for older students:
1. The American Association for Retired Persons' *Back-to-School Money Book: A Financial Aid Guide For Midlife and Older Women Seeking Education and Training,* single copies are free from AARP Fulfillment, 601 E Street, NW, Washington DC 20049 (request publication number D15400).
2. AARP's *Directory of Learning Opportunities for Older Persons.* This book is for older students who want to continue their education, but don't need college credit or a college degree. Single copies free. Request publication number D13973 from AARP Fulfillment, address above, or http://www.AARP.org.
2. Adult Learning Services, The College Board, 45 Columbus Avenue, New York, NY 10023.

Note: These are not scholarships sources, just helpful resources!

ARE YOU ONLY 25? 30?

Over 44% of all college students are 25 or older. Your best bet for financial aid (assuming you aren't a multi-millionaire) is that you will be filing your FAFSA as an independent student, thus only your own income and assets are assessed in calculating expected family contribution.

Chapter 24
A Few Words About Grad School

Graduate student aid falls into three main categories: Fellowships, assistantships and loans. Neither fellowships nor assistantships need to be repaid, however both usually require some sort of service (e.g., conducting research, working with faculty or teaching undergraduates). Most students rely on a combination of these three aid sources, however, Doctoral candidates are most likely to receive fellowships and assistantships, Master's students are most likely to receive a balance of assistantships and loans, and professional students are most likely to receive loans.

Further analysis of graduate student aid shows that of non-doctoral students, those in law, medicine and business have the largest loans. Those in engineering and the natural sciences receive the largest assistantships, and those in the natural sciences, medicine and the social sciences receive the largest fellowships. Similarly, of Doctoral students, those in medicine have the largest loans, those in engineering and the natural sciences receive the largest assistantships, and those in the natural sciences and the humanities receive the largest fellowships.

70% OF ALL GRADUATE AID

To learn where 70% of all graduate aid is, go back to the beginning of this book. First, you must enhance your eligibility for aid. The lessons in Chapters 4 through 7 are as applicable to graduate students as they are to undergrads. Second, review Chapter 10 and become familiar with federal sources of aid: Stafford Loans, Perkins Loans and Work-Study. If your future is in a medical field, add Chapter 20 to your reading. And, if all else fails, investigate the commercial loan sources listed in Chapter 7. **NOTE:** Graduate students are not eligible for Pell Grants or SEOGs.

3% OF ALL GRADUATE AID

For 3% of all graduate aid, check with your home state. Alabama, Alaska, Arizona, Arkansas, California, Colorado, Delaware, DC, Florida, Idaho, Iowa, Kansas, Louisiana, Maine, Maryland, Michigan, Mississippi, Nevada, New Mexico, New York, North Carolina, Ohio, Oklahoma, Pennsylvania, Texas, Utah, Vermont, Virginia, Washington, West Virginia, and Wisconsin offer $28 million in need-based aid and $36 million in non need-based aid. This money is not evenly distributed among the states. For example, New York alone awards $12.7 million to graduate students!

Also, many of these opportunities are sharply restricted in terms of major field of study (e.g., medicine, law, dentistry) or population group which benefits (e.g., minority). Furthermore students must usually enroll at an in-state school.

10% OF ALL GRADUATE AID

About 10% of all graduate aid is dispersed throughout this book. For instance, if you get a commission in the military and are willing to extend your period of service, you may qualify for graduate training. Employer-paid tuition and cooperative education (Chapter 12) are also rich in graduate opportunities. And you'll find more in Chapters 21 and 22.

12% OF ALL GRADUATE AID

For 12% of all graduate aid you must talk to your department chair. Here is how these people can help you:

- With departmental fellowships and grants. These are the most prestigious forms of aid and require very little from you in return.
- With graduate assistantships. Consider this an apprenticeship. While you have to work (quite a bit) for your money, the experience will look wonderful on your Curriculum Vitae (the academic version of a resume).
- With internships and summer jobs. With any luck, you may even find work you can turn into your thesis or dissertation.
- With employment funded by a grant. In most instances, the professor gets the grant, but will need grad students to help count chromosomes, wash test tubes, show slides, or lead discussion groups.

In graduate school, the committee that decides on admission also decides on these departmental awards. To better your chances for both, get to know the faculty. After you apply for admission, make appointments to meet professors in your area of interest. If it's relevant, send them a copy of your undergraduate thesis (or a research paper). Visit their classrooms. Observe their teaching styles. Be humble. And remember, unless you're applying to professional schools (law, medicine, business, engineering), your most important consideration should be to find a professor with whom you want to work. The reputation of the university is secondary to the reputation of the individual departments.

You might also consider going to work for a university. Many schools discount tuition for full-time employees, and while it may take you a few extra years to get through the program, you won't have a huge debt burden when you're through.

1% OF ALL GRADUATE AID

That you have to discover yourself. Through research. The best bet starting points for research: two publications put out by the Foundation Center and one by the Oryx Press. We don't recommend you buy these references. They are expensive. But do locate them in the reference room of the library and spend some time looking through them.

1. The Foundation Center's current *Foundation Directory.*
2. The Foundation Center's current *Foundation Grants to Individuals.*
3. The Oryx Press' current *Directory of Grants in the Humanities.*

4% OF ALL GRADUATE AID

All Disciplines

Request *A Selected List of Fellowship and Other Support Opportunities for Advanced Education* from The Publications Office, National Science Foundation, 4201 Wilson Blvd., Arlington, VA 22230. It contains information on opportunities for US citizens and foreign nationals in many fields of study (including the humanities, social sciences, engineering, physical sciences, math, and life sciences).

Communicative Disorders

For students pursuing master's degrees in audiology or speech pathology from institutions in the US, Canada or Mexico. 30 awards of $2,500 per year. By 1 April. For more information, send SASE to Sertoma World Headquarters, Communicative Disorders Scholarship, 1912 East Meyer Blvd., Kansas City, MO 64132.

Engineering and Science

The Fellowship Office of the National Research Council administers a variety of predoctoral and dissertation fellowships. For program brochures, write The National Research Council, Office of Scientific and Engineering Personnel, Fellowship Programs, 2101 Constitution Ave., Washington, DC 20418.

Engineering and Science

Nat'l Defense Science and Engineering Graduate Fellowship Program sponsored by the Dept. of Defense. Three year fellowships leading to graduate degree in science or engineering. Full tuition plus stipend. No service obligation. NDSEG Fellowship Program, 200 Park Drive #211, Research Triangle Park, NC 27709, Attn: Dr. George Outterson, http://www.battelle.org/ndseg/ndseg.html.

Engineering and Science

Fellowships. College seniors for graduate study. US citizenship required. GPA must be 3.0/4.0. Most on a work-study basis. Spend summer vacation working at Hughes Aircraft Co. Tuition, fees, stipend, travel and relocation expenses, salary for summer and other periods of full-time work. Hughes Aircraft Company, PO Box 80028, Bldg. C1/B168, Los Angeles, CA 90080-0028. (310) 568-6711.

Humanities

Eighty awards (one-year only) for students entering a program leading to a Ph.D. in preparation for careers of teaching and scholarship in the humanities. Tuition plus $13,750 stipend. Applications must be requested by mid-December. To get an application, you must provide the following information: Full name, mailing address, city and state, telephone number, location in March 1997, undergraduate institution, undergraduate major, year of graduation, intended discipline in graduate school, and e-mail address (if available). Send all this to: Mellon Fellowships, Woodrow Wilson National Fellowship Foundation, CN 5329, Princeton, NJ 08543-5329.

International Business

Some student fellowships. 35 awards. Funded through schools. For school list, write: Office of International Studies Branch, Department of Education, Rm. 3054, ROB-3, 400 Maryland Avenue, SW, Washington, DC 20202.

International Exchange

Possession of BA degree. Live and study abroad as a Fulbright student. 800 students go to 100 nations. Write IIE, US Student Programs, 809 UN Plaza, New York, NY 10017. (212) 984-5330.

Languages and Teaching

Graduate fellowships for foreign language and area studies. Funded through schools. Schools select students. Tuition and stipends. Direct inquiries to university of choice; if necessary, for school list, write: Center for Internat'l Education (FLAS), US Dept.. of Education, Washington, DC 20202-5331.

Law

The Access Group and Lawloans both offer Bar Examination Loans of up to $5,000 to help students pay for living expenses and a bar review course. While the rates can be high, students who can't get a loan from their parents or an advance from their future employer often have no other choice. After all, what bank is going to lend money to a person with no income and $60,000 in law school debt? You can call the Access Group at 800/282-1550 or Lawloans at 800/366-5626

Librarianship

Library and Human Resource Development Program. Funded through schools. For school list and copy of *Financial Assistance for Library and Information Studies,* write: Discretionary Library Programs Division, OERI, Dept. of Education, 555 New Jersey Avenue, NW, Washington, DC 20208-5571.

Marine Sciences

Marine Sciences and Marine Affairs. John A. Knauss Marine Policy Federal Fellows Program for enrolled graduate/professional students. Request brochure from National Sea Grant College Program Office, Attn: Fellowship Director, 1315 East West Highway, Silver Spring, MD 20910.

Music

The Musicological Society offers 5 dissertation fellowships per year. Twelve-month stipend (nonrenewable) of $10,000. Application forms from AMS 50, Department of Music, Smith College, Northampton, MA 01063. By October 1.

National Needs Areas

Stipends of $14,000 to enhance teaching and research in designated academic needs areas (examples—math, agricultural science, and foreign languages). These awards go to graduate students of superior ability who demonstrate financial need. $25 million is distributed through 84 different schools. Funding is tenuous. For school list, write Division of Higher Educational Incentive Programs, Office of Post-secondary Education, Department of Education, Rm. 3022, 400 Maryland Avenue SW, Washington, DC 20202-5339.

Professional Students

Loans for MBAs (800/366-6227), Med School (800/858-5050) and Law School (800/282-1550).

Science, Social Science, Math, Engineering

Graduate study in sciences, social sciences, mathematics and engineering. Three separate competitions: NSF Graduate Fellowships, Minority Graduate Fellowships and Women in Engineering and Computer Science Awards. Three years of support. Approximately $14,400 per year. 750 new fellows yearly. For more information (and a catalogue), write Oak Ridge Associated Universities, PO Box 3010, Oak Ridge, TN 37831). Deadline is early Nov.

Space-Related Science and Engineering, Aerospace Research

1. Summer programs and renewable graduate school awards of up to $22,000. For more information: Graduate Student Researchers Program, Higher Education Branch, Education Division, NASA Headquarters, Mail Code FEH, Washington, DC 20546, http://spacelink.msfc.nasa.gov.
2. Graduate and doctoral fellowships at affiliated schools. For more information: Space Grant College and Fellowship Program, University Programs Branch, NASA Headquarters, Mail Code FEH, Washington, DC, 20546.

ADDITIONAL RESOURCES

The National Association of Graduate and Professional Students has an active and extensive web site: http://www.nagps.org/NAGPS/nagps-hp.html. You should also pick up the current edition of Dr. Robert Peter's comprehensive graduate student guide, *Getting What You Came For.*

Chapter 25
A Treasure Chest of Tips

In an ideal world, the sound of the budget axe one year would be replaced by the burble of flowing federal funds the next. Unfortunately, that's not likely. Students today must cope with aid funding that doesn't keep pace with rising tuition costs. For these students, the slogan is "know more about every aspect of financial aid or dig deeper." To save you the purchase of a new shovel, here is a summary of the skills you, as a student today, must master.

Selecting a College (I)

When picking a college, go beyond the normal search criteria, such as majors offered, academic reputation, and distance from home, and inquire about innovative tuition aid features. These may include matching scholarships, sibling scholarships, guaranteed cost plans, installment plans, special middle income assistance programs, tuition remission for high grades, etc.

See Chapter 9.

Selecting a College (II)

All factors being equal, pick colleges most likely to offer you a financial aid package rich in grants you don't have to repay. Such a package is a lot better than one made up of loans which will saddle you with a repayment burden for many years after graduation. Best bet: Any school in which your academic record places you in the upper 25% of the profile of the incoming freshman class.

See Chapters 7 and 9.

Selecting a College (III)

Send applications to two colleges of equal merit. If you get accepted by both, you might be able to play one against the other in securing a more favorable package.

See Chapters 7 and 9.

Try the External Degree Route

Win a sheepskin without ever leaving home or job. Such a diploma will cost less in money and time than if it had been earned through campus attendance. External degrees offer academic credit for documented learning and experience you have already acquired, and couples these with formal assessments.

See Chapter 7.

Do Four Years Work in Three

You must attend summer school, but the compressed time will save you the "inflationary increase" of the fourth year. On a similar note, try to avoid taking extra years to get through college. Fewer and fewer students are graduating in four years...costing them a whole extra year's tuition.

See Chapter 7.

Start at a Community College

Work hard. Get good grades. Transfer to a solid four-year institution. This way, you pick up the halo of a prestige diploma at half the cost.

See Chapter 7.

Understand How Need Analysis Works

By knowing the formulas, the shrewd family can present its financial picture in such a way as to obtain a more favorable need analysis. This isn't unlike the method used for presenting one's financial picture to the IRS so as to qualify for the smallest possible tax liability.

See Chapters 6 and 7.

Try Some "What If?" Calculations

But first, learn how need analysis works. A typical "what if": Is this a good time for mom or dad to finish their college work, along with son and daughter? Or will it be more advantageous, financially, for your parent to go back to work and help with expenses? You'll be surprised at the dollar figures generated by "what if" drills.

See Chapter 7.

Don't Pass Up the Entitlement Programs

Billions in low-interest, subsidized federal student loans go unused each year simply because students think they are ineligible, don't bother to go through the paper work hassle, or just don't know about the program.

See Chapter 10 and *Loans and Grants From Uncle Sam* (inside back cover).

Cash Flow (I)

Search for a low-interest, private loan. Numerous states have set up loan authorities which float tax-exempt bonds to raise student loan money. And colleges themselves have received permission to issue such bonds. At the same time, private banks are becoming more innovative in sponsoring combination savings/lending plans. Keep an eye out for these developments. They can help middle-income families with the cash flow problem of paying for college.

See Chapters 6, 7, and 9.

Cash Flow (II)

Go to college on the house. Many home owners have accumulated large amounts of equity in their houses and they want to put it to work. Your strategy: Releasing this equity either through a line of credit or through refinancing the first mortgage.

See Chapters 7 and 9.

Negotiate With the Financial Aid Administrator

The FAA will present you with a package of assistance that should, in theory, cover the difference between what college costs and what your family can contribute. If you feel the college really wants you, because you are a brain or an athlete or the child of an alum or can help it meet a geographic or minority quota, you may want to ask the FAA about improving the package. Your objective: To increase the grant component (money that doesn't have to be repaid) and reduce the loan component (money you must repay).

See Chapters 6, 7, and 9.

Try for an Academic Scholarship

Over 1200 colleges offer academic scholarships to students with a B average and SAT scores of 900 or more. Middle income folks take notice: Most of these scholarships are not based on financial need. If you are just outside the SAT eligibility range for one of these awards, take a good SAT preparation course. It may raise your scores enough to enter the winner's circle.

See Chapter 18 and *The A's and B's of Academic Scholarships* (inside back cover).

Go the Cooperative Education Route

Over 900 colleges offer co-op education programs. Alternate formal study with periods of career-related work. Earn up to $7,000 per year during the work phase. It may take an extra year to win the degree, but it will be easier on the pocketbook.

See Chapter 12 and *Earn & Learn* (inside back cover).

Athletic Student Aid

We aren't talking about the "Body by Nautilus, Mind by Mattel" tackle who can do 40 yards in 4 seconds. Husky U. will find that person. We're talking about students who are better than average in a variety of sports, ranging from tennis to golf to lacrosse. A great many colleges seek people who can be developed into varsity material. The rewards come in two forms: outright scholarships or "improved" financial aid packages.

See Chapter 19.

Acceleration

Can you get credit for a semester or a year of college work? You can through the Advanced Placement Program or by enrolling in college courses in high school. When credits can cost as much as $300 each, receiving tuition credit for academic credit leaves money in the bank.

See Chapters 7.

Be An Accurate, Early Bird

Be as accurate as possible in filling out financial aid forms. Submit them as early as you can. When resources are tight, it's first-come, first-served. Those who must resubmit their forms and those who are slow in applying come in at the end of the line. By then, all the money is gone.

See Chapters 6 and 7.

Check the Military Offerings

Reserve enlistments are especially attractive. For a hitch in the National Guard you can pick up a state benefit, a federal bonus, partial loan forgiveness, drill pay, sergeant stripes (if you also participate in ROTC), and in some cases, tuition remission at the state university. And these are not "either/or" opportunities. You can have most of them, or all of them.

See Chapter 13.

Take Advantage of Teacher Mania

Individual colleges, most states, and Uncle Sam all have loan forgiveness programs for prospective teachers. Go this route and your education will cost you very little. You teach Ohm's law for four years to pay off the obligation. You pick up a little maturity, a lot of patience. You contribute to the well-being of hundreds of scholars-to-be. And you're still young enough to begin a different career if teaching is not for you.

See Chapters 9 and 11.

Sacrifice

You may have to give up a few luxuries: Cancelling your pet's Beverly Hills grooming sessions can save you $3,200 per dog per year; using a Volkswagen instead of your Lear jet can save you $540 per tank of gas.

APPENDIX 1

Family Contribution for Dependent Students (1997/98 Academic Year)

Parent's Contribution from Income

1. Parents' Adjusted Gross Income .... $ _____
2. Parents' Untaxed Social Security Benefits .... $ _____
3. Parents' Aid to Families With Dependent Children Benefits. .... $ _____
4. Parents' Other Nontaxable Income. This may include child support received, worker's compensation, disability payments, welfare benefits, tax-exempt interest income, housing, food and living allowances for military, clergy or others. .... $ _____
5. Deductible IRA, KEOGH, and 401(k) payments made by parents. .... $ _____
6. **Total Income.** Add Lines 1 through 5. .... $ _____
7. US and State Income Taxes paid. .... $ _____
8. Social Security Taxes paid .... $ _____
9. Child Support paid by you for another child. .... $ _____
10. Income Protection Allowance from Table A. .... $ _____
11. Employment Expense Allowance. If both parents work, enter 35% of the lower income or $2,700, whichever is less. If your family has a single head of household who works, enter 35% of that income or $2,700, whichever is less. .... $ _____
12. **Total Allowances.** Add Lines 7 through 11. .... $ _____
13. **Parents' Available Income.** Line 6 minus Line 12 .... $ _____

Parents Contribution from Assets*

14. Cash and Bank Accounts. .... $ _____
15. Other Real estate, investments, stocks, bonds, trust funds, commodities, precious metals (less any investment debt). .... $ _____
16. Business and/or Commercial Farm Net Worth from Table B. .... $ _____
17. **Total Assets.** Add Lines 14 through 16. .... $ _____
18. Asset Protection Allowance. From Table C. .... $ _____
19. Discretionary Net Worth. Line 17 minus Line 18. .... $ _____
20. **CONTRIBUTION FROM ASSETS.** Multiply Line 19 by 12%. If negative, enter $0. .... $ _____

Parental Contribution

21. Adjusted Available Income. Add Lines 13 and 20. .... $ _____
22. **PARENT CONTRIBUTION.** From Table D. If negative, enter 0. ... $ _____
23. Number in College Adjustment. Divide Line 22 by the number in college (at least half-time) at the same time. Quotient is the contribution for each student. .... $ _____

Student's Contribution from Income

24. Student's Adjusted Gross Income. ....$ _____
25. Untaxed Social Security Benefits ....$ _____
26. Other Untaxed income and benefits. See Line 4. Also include cash support paid on your behalf from non-custodial parent, or any other person ....$ _____
27. Deductible IRA payments made by student ....$ _____
28. Total Income. Add lines 24 through 27. ....$ _____
29. US Income Taxes paid. ....$ _____
30. State Income Taxes paid. ....$ _____
31. Social Security Taxes paid. ....$ _____
32. Income Protection Allowance. Enter $1,750. ....$ _____
33. Total Allowances. Add Lines 29 through 32. ....$ _____
34. Students Available Income. Line 28 minus Line 33. ....$ _____
35. **STUDENT'S CONTRIBUTION FROM INCOME.** Multiply Line 34 by 50%. . ...$ _____

Student's Contribution from Assets*

36. Add all of student's assets—cash, savings, trusts, investments, real estate (less any investment debt)....................................$ _____
37. **STUDENT'S CONTRIBUTION FROM ASSETS.** Take 35% of Line 36. ....$ _____

Family Contribution

38. If one student is in college, add lines 22, 35, and 37. ....$ _____
39. If two or more students are in college at the same time, add for each, Lines 23, 35, and 37. ....$ _____

*Contribution from student and parent assets will equal $0 if Parents' AGI (Line 1) is less than $50,000 and the family is eligible to file a 1040A, 1040 EZ, or no tax return at all. If you want to get a rough estimate of your EFC under the Institutional Methodology, ignore this $50,000 rule and include home equity in the value of your assets (Line 17).

APPENDIX 2

Family Contribution for Independent Students with Dependents (1997/98 Academic Year)

Contribution from Income (Student's and Spouse's)

1. Student's (and Spouse's) Adjusted Gross Income. .... $ _____
2. Student's (and Spouse's) Untaxed Social Security Benefits .... $ _____
3. Student's (and Spouse's) Aid to Families With Dependent Children Benefits. .... $ _____
4. Student's (and Spouse's) Other Nontaxable Income. This may include child support received, worker's compensation, disability payments, interest on tax-exempt bonds, welfare benefits, cash support from others, housing, food and living allowances for military, clergy or others. .... $ _____
5. Deductible IRA, KEOGH, 401 (k) Payments made by Student (and Spouse). .... $ _____
6. **Total Income.** Add Lines 1 through 5. .... $ _____
7. US and State Income Taxes paid. .... $ _____
8. Social Security Taxes paid .... $ _____
9. Child support paid by you for another child. .... $ _____
10. Income Protection Allowance from Table A. .... $ _____
11. Employment Expense Allowance. If both student and spouse work, enter 35% of the lower income or $2,700, whichever is less; If student qualifies as head of household, enter 35% of income or $2,700, whichever is less. .... $ _____
12. **Total Allowances.** Add Lines 7 through 11. .... $ _____
13. **Available Income.** Line 6 minus Line 12. .... $ _____

Contribution from Assets (Student's and Spouse's)*

14. Cash and Bank Accounts. .... $ _____
15. Other Real estate, investments, stocks, bonds, trust funds, commodities, precious metals (less investment debt). .... $ _____
16. Business and/or Commercial Farm Net Worth from Table B. .... $ _____
17. **Total Assets.** Add Lines 14 through 16. .... $ _____
18. Asset Protection Allowance. From Table E. .... $ _____
19. Discretionary Net Worth. Line 17 minus Line 18. .... $ _____
20. **CONTRIBUTION FROM ASSETS.** Multiply Line 19 by 12%. If the result is a negative value, enter $0. .... $ _____
21. Adjusted Available Income. Add Line 13 and Line 20. .... $ _____
22. **TOTAL CONTRIBUTION.** From Table D. .... $ _____
23. Number in College Adjustment. Divide Line 22 by the number in college (at least half-time) at the same time. Quotient is the contribution for each student. .... $ _____

*Contribution from assets will equal $0 if Student and Spouse AGI (Line 1) is less than $50,000 and the student (and spouse) were eligible to file a 1040A or 1040EZ or no tax return at all. If you want to get a rough estimate of your EFC under the Institutional Methodology, ignore this $50,000 rule and include home equity in the value of your assets (Line 17).

APPENDIX 3

Family Contribution for Independent Students without Dependents other than a Spouse (1997/98 Academic Year)

Contribution from Income (Student's and Spouse's)

1. Student's (and Spouse's) Adjusted Gross Income. ....$ _____
2. Student's (and Spouse's) Untaxed Social Security Benefits ....$ _____
3. Student's (and Spouse's) Welfare Benefits. ....$ _____
4. Student's (and Spouse's) Other Nontaxable Income. This may include child support received, worker's compensation, disability payments, interest on tax-exempt bonds, welfare benefits, cash support from others, housing, and living allowances for military, clergy or others. ....$ _____
5. Deductible IRA, KEOGH, 401 (k) Payments made by Student (and Spouse). ....$ _____
6. **Total Income.** Add Lines 1 through 5. ....$ _____
7. US Income Taxes paid. ....$ _____
8. State Income Taxes paid ....$ _____
9. Social Security Taxes paid. ....$ _____
10. Income Protection Allowance of $3,000 for single students or married students if both are enrolled in college at least half time; $6,000 for married students if only one is enrolled at least half-time.$ _____
11. Employment Expense Allowance. If the student is single, enter $0. If the student is married and both the student and spouse are working, enter 35% of the lower income or $2,700, whichever is less. Otherwise enter $0 ....$ _____
12. **Total Allowances.** Add Lines 7 through 11. ....$ _____
13. **Available Income.** Line 6 minus Line 12. ....$ _____
14. **Contribution from Income.** Take 50% of Line 13. ....$ _____

Contribution from Assets (Student's and Spouse's)*

15. Cash and Bank Accounts. ....$ _____
16. Other Real estate, investments, stocks, bonds, trust funds, commodities, precious metals (less any investment debt). ....$ _____
17. Business and/or Commercial Farm Net Worth from Table B. ....$ _____
18. **Total Assets.** Add Lines 15 through 17. ....$ _____
19. Asset Protection Allowance. From Table E. ....$ _____
20. Discretionary Net Worth. Line 18 minus Line 19. ....$ _____
21. **CONTRIBUTION FROM ASSETS.** Multiply Line 20 by 35%. If negative, adjust to 0. ....$ _____
22. **TOTAL CONTRIBUTION.** Add Line 14 and Line 21. ....$ _____
23. Number in College Adjustment. Divide Line 22 by the number in college (at least half-time) at the same time. Quotient is the contribution for each student. ....$ _____

* Contribution from assets will equal $0 if Student (and Spouse) AGI (Line 1) is less than $50,000 and the student (and spouse) are eligible to file a 1040A or 1040EZ or no tax return at all. If you want to get a rough estimate of your EFC under the Institutional Methodology, ignore this $50,000 rule and include home equity in the value of your assets (Line 18).

REFERENCE TABLES

Table A—Income Protection Allowance

Family Members (Including Student)	Allowance
2	$11,750
3	14,630
4	18,070
5	21,320
6	24,940
Each Additional	2,810

Note: *For each student over one in college, subtract $2,000 from the appropriate maintenance allowance.*

Table B—Adjustment of Business/Farm Net Worth

Net Worth of Business/Farm	Adjustment
To $85,000	40% of Net Worth
$85,001 to $250,000	$34,000, plus 50% of NW over $85,000
$250,001 to $420,000	$116,500, plus 60% of NW over $250,000
$420,001 or more	$218,500 plus 100% of NW over $420,000

Table C—Asset Protection Allowance, Dependent Student

Age of Older Parent	Two-Parent Family	One Parent Family
40-44	$37,300	$26,000
45-49	42,400	29,000
50-54	48,300	32,700
55-59	55,900	36,900
60-64	65,400	42,300
65 plus	72,400	46,100

Table D—Parent Contribution

Adjusted Available Income (AAI)	Parent Contribution
To minus $3,409	-$750 (negative figure)
Minus $3,409 to plus $10,500	22% of AAI
$10,501 to $13,200	$2,310 plus 25% of AAI over $10,500
$13,201 to $15,900	$2,985 plus 29% of AAI over $13,200
$15,901 to $18,500	$3,768 plus 34% of AAI over $15,900
$18,501 to $21,200	$4,652 plus 40% of AAI over $18,500
$21,201 or more	$5,732 plus 47% of AAI over $21,200

Table E—Asset Protection Allowance, Independent Student

Age	Single	Married
25 & Under	$ 0	$ 0
26	1,700	2,400
29	6,600	9,500
32	11,600	16,600
35	16,600	23,700
38	21,600	30,800
40	24,900	35,500
50	31,200	45,900
65	46,100	72,400

144